THE PLACE OF TOLERANCE IN ISLAM

THE PLACE OF TOLERANCE
IN ISLAM

KHALED ABOU EL FADL

EDITED BY JOSHUA COHEN AND IAN LAGUE
FOR *BOSTON REVIEW*

,

BEACON PRESS
BOSTON

BEACON PRESS
25 Beacon Street
Boston, Massachusetts 02108-2892
www.beacon.org

Beacon Press books
are published under the auspices of
the Unitarian Universalist Association of Congregations.

06 05 04 03 02   8 7 6 5 4 3 2

This book is printed on acid-free paper that meets the uncoated paper
ANSI/NISO specifications for permanence as revised in 1992.

Composition by Wilsted & Taylor Publishing Services

Library of Congress Cataloging-in-Publication Data
Abou El Fadl, Khaled.
       The place of tolerance in Islam / Khaled Abou El Fadl ; edited by Joshua
Cohen and Ian Lague for Boston review.
       p.   cm.
Includes bibliographical references.
       ISBN 0-8070-0229-1 (pbk. : alk. paper)
       1. Religious tolerance—Islam.   2. Liberty of conscience (Islam)
3. Islam—Relations.   I. Cohen, Joshua.   II. Lague, Ian.   III. Boston review
(Cambridge, Mass. : 1982)   IV. Title.
       BP171.5 .A28 2002
       297.2'72—dc21

                                                                    2002008425

CONTENTS

EDITORS' PREFACE

JOSHUA COHEN AND IAN LAGUE

Since September 11, Western discussions of Islam have typically been conducted through a contest of caricatures. Some analysts present Islamic extremism as a product of a "clash of civilizations" that pits Eastern despotism against Western individualism. Others see such extremism as a grim "blowback" of America's cold-war foreign policy. Engagement with Muslim faith commonly takes the form of simplistic pronouncements about "essence" of Islam: Osama bin Laden either represents the true message of the Prophet or corrupts a "religion of peace."

As Khaled Abou El Fadl points out, these discussions are driven more by Western concerns—"are Muslims dangerous or not?"—than by a serious effort to understand Islam and the place of toleration and moral decency in its conception of a proper human life. In his lead essay for this volume, Abou El Fadl opens such a conversation. A professor at UCLA, theorist of Islamic law, and prominent critic of Islamic puritanism, Abou El Fadl works to reclaim the "moral trust" of Islam by recovering the Qur'an's universal principles from the historical and social context in which the text was received. He interprets Qur'anic verses about the treatment of women and non-Muslims in light of scriptural passages that call for mercy, kindness, and justice, and that emphasize the essentially plural nature of the human community.

Abou El Fadl's engagement with these theological issues is enriched by a broad historical perspective. He points out that intolerant sects have traditionally been marginalized by Islamic civilization. But Islam, he argues, currently faces a crisis of religious authority owing to the political exploitation of Islamic symbols and the stagnation of civic and economic life in Muslim societies. That crisis has facilitated the rise of puritanical sects who interpret the Qur'an literally and ahistorically. Abou El Fadl acknowledges that the Qur'an itself, like other ancient religious texts, cannot forestall such interpretations: interpretation is an act for which readers must take moral responsibility. In the end, religious texts provide rich "possibilities for meaning, not inevitabilities," so "the text will morally enrich the reader, but only if the reader will morally enrich the text."

While a majority of respondents accept Abou El Fadl's critique of Islamic puritanism, they take issue with this general conception of the debate and with his specific arguments. Some respondents contend that Abou El Fadl's brand of Islam will only appeal to Westerners and students in "liberal divinity schools" and that religious dialogue in the Muslim world will be useless unless it is accompanied by dramatic social and political reform. Other respondents argue that theological debates are irrelevant and that the focus should be on the Western sabotage of such reforms. A different group of respondents criticizes these same policies as part of an exploitative program of Western secularization, and argues that calls for Islamic "tolerance" betray the Qur'anic injunction for Muslims to struggle against their oppressors.

These disagreements demonstrate that a discussion of tolerance in Islam cannot take place in isolation from debates about the distribution of political power and economic resources. But they also underscore the enduring challenge posed by religious morality in a pluralistic age: how can we retain the richness and intensity of conviction provided by a religious outlook while participating in what Abou El Fadl calls "a collective enterprise of goodness" that cuts across confessional differences?

1

THE PLACE OF TOLERANCE IN ISLAM

KHALED ABOU EL FADL

The terrorist attacks on New York City and the Pentagon have focused public attention on the state of Muslim theology. For most Americans, the utter indifference to the value of human life and the unmitigated hostility to the United States shown by some Muslims came as a great shock. Others were confirmed in their belief that we face a great struggle between civilizations. Islamic values, they say, are fundamentally at odds with Western liberal values. The terrorist attacks are symptomatic of a clash between Judeo-Christian civilization, with its values of individual freedom, pluralism, and secularism, and an amoral, un-Westernized, so-called "authentic Islam." Indeed, Islamic civilization is associated with the ideas of collective rights, individual duties, legalism, despotism, and intolerance that we associated with our former civilizational rival, the Soviet bloc. We seem to project onto the other everything we like to think that we are not.

This intellectual trap is easy to fall into when we deal with the theology of Osama bin Laden, the Taliban, the Wahhabis of Saudi Arabia, and the Jihad organization. The theologically based attitudes of these Muslim puritans are fundamentally at odds not only with a Western way of life but also with the very idea of an international society or the notion of universal human values. They display an intolerant exclusiveness and a belligerent supremacy vis-à-vis the other. According to their theologies, Islam is the only way of life, and must be pursued regardless of its impact on the rights and well-being of others. The straight path (*al-sirat al-mustaqim*) is fixed, they say, by a system of divine laws (*shari'a*) that trump any moral considerations or ethical values that are not fully codified in the law. God is manifested through a set of determinate legal commands that specify the right way to act in virtually all circumstances. The sole purpose of human life on earth is to realize the divine manifestation by dutifully and faithfully implementing God's law. Morality itself begins and ends in the mechanics and technicalities of Islamic law (though different schools of Islamic law understand the content of those laws differently).

A life devoted to compliance with this legal code is considered inherently superior to all others, and the followers of any other way are considered either infidels (*kuffar*), hypocrites (*munafiqun*), or iniquitous (*fasiqun*). Anchored in the security and assuredness of a determinable law, it becomes fairly easy to differentiate between the rightly-guided and the misguided. The rightly-guided obey the law; the misguided either deny, attempt to dilute, or argue about the law. Naturally, the rightly-guided are superior because they have

God on their side. The Muslim puritans imagine that God's perfection and immutability are fully attainable on earth—as if God's perfection had been deposited in the divine law, and, by giving effect to this law, we could create a social order that mirrors divine truth. By attaching themselves to the Supreme Being, puritan groups are able to claim a self-righteous perfectionism that easily slips into a pretense of supremacy.

Extremism in Islamic History

Perhaps all firmly held systems of belief, especially those founded on religious conviction, are in some way supremacist: believers are understood to have some special virtue that distinguishes them from adherents of other faiths. But the supremacist creed of the puritan groups is distinctive and uniquely dangerous. The supremacist thinking of Muslim puritans has a powerful nationalist component, which is strongly oriented toward cultural and political dominance. These groups are not satisfied with living according to their own dictates, but are actively dissatisfied with all alternative ways of life. They do not merely seek self-empowerment but aggressively seek to disempower, dominate, or destroy others. The crux of the matter is that all lives lived outside the law are considered an offense against God that must be actively resisted and fought.

The existence of Muslim puritanism is hardly surprising. Most religious systems have suffered at one time or another from absolutist extremism, and Islam is no exception. Within the first century of Islam, religious extremists known as the Khawarij (literally, the secessionists) slaughtered a large number of Muslims and non-Muslims, and were even responsible for the assassination of the Prophet's cousin and companion, the Caliph Ali b. Abi Talib. The descendants of the Khawarij exist today in Oman and Algeria, but after centuries of bloodshed, they became moderates if not pacifists. Similarly, the Qaramites and Assassins, for whom terror became a raison d'être, earned unmitigated infamy in the writings of Muslim historians, theologians, and jurists. Again, after centuries of bloodshed, these two groups learned moderation, and they continue to exist in small numbers in North Africa and Iraq. The essential lesson taught by Islamic history is that extremist groups are ejected from the mainstream of Islam; they are marginalized, and eventually treated as heretical aberrations to the Islamic message.

But Islam is now living through a major shift, unlike any it has experienced in the past. The Islamic civilization has crumbled, and the traditional institutions that once sustained and propagated Islamic orthodoxy—and marginalized Islamic extremism—have been dismantled. Traditionally, Islamic epistemology tolerated and even celebrated divergent opinions and schools of thought. The guardians of the Islamic tradition were the jurists (*fuqaha*), whose legitimacy rested largely on their semi-independence from a decentralized political system, and their dual function of representing the interests of the state to the laity and the interests of the laity to the state.

But in Muslim countries today, the state has grown extremely powerful and meddlesome, and is centralized in ways that were inconceivable two centuries ago. In the vast majority of Muslim countries, the state now controls the private religious endowments (*awqaf*) that once sustained the juristic class. Moreover, the state has co-opted the clergy, and transformed them into its salaried employees. This transformation has reduced the clergy's legitimacy, and produced a profound vacuum in religious authority. Hence, there is a state of virtual anarchy in modern Islam: it is not clear who speaks with authority on religious issues. Such a state of virtual religious anarchy is perhaps not problematic in secular societies where religion is essentially reduced to a private matter. But where religion remains central to the dynamics of public legitimacy and cultural meaning, the question of who represents the voice of God is of central significance.

PURITANISM AND MODERN ISLAM

It would be wrong to say that fanatic supremacist groups such as al-Qaeda or al-Jihad organizations now fill the vacuum of authority in contemporary Islam. Though they are obviously able to commit highly visible acts of violence that command the public stage, fanatic groups remain sociologically and intellectually marginal in Islam. Still, they are extreme manifestations of more prevalent intellectual and theological currents in modern Islam.

Fanatic groups derive their theological premises from the intolerant puritanism of the Wahhabi and Salafi creeds. Wahhabism was founded by the eighteenth-century evangelist Muhammad ibn 'Abd al-Wahhab in the Arabian Peninsula. 'Abd al-Wahhab sought to rid Islam of the corruptions that he believed had crept into the religion. He advocated a strict literalism in which the text became the sole source of legitimate authority, and displayed an extreme hostility to intellectualism, mysticism, and any sectarian divisions within Islam. According to the Wahhabi creed, it was imperative to return to a presumed pristine, simple, straightforward Islam, which could be entirely reclaimed by literal implementation of the commands of the Prophet, and by strict adherence to correct ritual practice. Importantly, Wahhabism rejected any attempt to interpret the divine law historically or contextually, with attendant possibilities of reinterpretation under changed circumstances. It treated the vast majority of Islamic history as a corruption of the true and authentic Islam. Furthermore, Wahhabism narrowly defined orthodoxy, and was extremely intolerant of any creed that contradicted its own.

In the late eighteenth century, the Al Sa'ud family united with the Wahhabi movement and rebelled against Ottoman rule in Arabia. The rebellions were very bloody because the Wahhabis indiscriminately slaughtered and terrorized Muslims and non-Muslims alike. Interestingly, mainstream jurists writing at the time, such as the Hanafi Ibn 'Abidin and the Maliki al-Sawi, branded the Wahhabis the modern day Khawarij of Islam, and condemned their fanaticism and intolerance.[1] In 1818, Egyptian forces under the leadership of Muhammad Ali defeated this rebellion, and Wahhabism seemed destined to become another fringe historical experience with no lasting impact on Islamic theology. But the Wahhabi creed was resuscitated in the early twentieth century under the leadership of 'Abd al-'Aziz ibn Sa'ud, who allied himself with Wahhabi militant rebels known as the Ikhwan, in the beginnings of what would become Saudi Arabia. Even with the formation of the Saudi state, Wahhabism remained a creed of limited influence until the mid-1970s when the sharp rise in oil prices, together with aggressive Saudi proselytizing, dramatically contributed to its wide dissemination in the Muslim world.

Wahhabism did not propagate itself as one school of thought or a particular orientation within Islam. Rather, it asserted itself as the orthodox "straight path" of Islam. By claiming literal fidelity to the Islamic text, it was able to make a credible claim to authenticity at a time when Islamic identity was contested. Moreover, the proponents of Wahhabism refused to be labeled or categorized as the followers of any particular figure including 'Abd al-Wahhab himself. Its proponents insisted that they were simply abiding by the dictates of *al-salaf al-salih* (the rightly-guided predecessors, namely the Prophet and his companions), and in doing so, Wahhabis were able to appropriate the symbolisms and categories of Salafism.

Ironically, Salafism was founded in the early twentieth century by al-Afghani, Muhammad Abduh, and Rashid Rida as a liberal theological orientation. To respond to the demands of modernity, they argued, Muslims needed to return to the original sources of the Qur'an and Sunnah (tradition of the Prophet), and engage in de novo interpretations of the text. By the 1970s, however, Wahhabism had succeeded in transforming Salafism from a liberal modernist orientation to a literalist, puritan, and conservative theology. The sharp rise in oil prices in 1975 enabled Saudi Arabia, the main proponent of Wahhabism, to disseminate the Wahhabi creed under a Salafi guise, which purported to revert back to the authentic fundamentals of religion uncorrupted by the accretions of historical practice. In reality, however, Saudi Arabia projected its own fairly conservative cultural practices onto the textual sources of Islam and went on to proselytize these projections as the embodiment of Islamic orthodoxy.

Despite its intolerance and rigidity, however, Wahhabism itself does not bear primary responsibility for the existence of terrorist groups in Islam today. To be sure, Wahhabism and its militant offshoots share both attitudinal and ideological orientations. Both insist on a normative particularism that is fundamentally text-centered; both reject the notion of universal human values; and both deal with the

other, however defined, in a functionalist and even opportunistic fashion. But Wahhabism is distinctively inward-
looking—although focused on power, it primarily asserts
power over other Muslims. This is consistent with its ob-
session with orthodoxy and correct ritualistic practice.
Militant puritan groups, however, are both introverted and
extroverted—they attempt to assert power against both
Muslims and non-Muslims. As populist movements, they
are a reaction to the disempowerment most Muslims have
suffered in the modern age at the hands of harshly despotic
governments, and at the hands of interventionist foreign
powers. These groups compensate for extreme feelings of
disempowerment by extreme and vulgar claims to power.
Fueled by supremacist and puritan theological creeds, their
symbolic acts of power become uncompromisingly fanatic
and violent.

THE THEOLOGY OF INTOLERANCE

Islamic puritans, whether of the Wahhabi or more militant
varieties, offer a set of textual references in support of their
exclusionary and intolerant theological orientation. For instance, they frequently cite the Qur'anic verse that states:
"O' you who believe, do not take the Jews and Christians as
allies. They are allies of each other, and he amongst you who
becomes their ally is one of them. Verily, God does not
guide the unjust."[2] Wahhabi and militant puritanism read
this and similar Qur'anic verses literally and ahistorically,

and therefore reach highly exclusionary conclusions. For example, while Muslims may elicit the support or aid of non-Muslims over particular issues when the self-interests of Muslims so require, they may not befriend or share the normative values of non-Muslims. This orientation often demands the performance of symbolic acts, which aim to distinguish Muslims from non-Muslims—for instance, dressing in a particular way or marking non-Muslims with distinctive symbols.

Islamic puritanism also often invokes the Qur'anic verse asserting that, "whomsoever follows a religion other than Islam this will not be accepted from him, and in the Hereafter he will be among the losers."[3] This verse is invoked in arguing that the theology and rituals of Islam are the exclusive path to salvation. Moreover, a mere testament of faith or a general act of submission to God is insufficient to attain salvation in the Hereafter; rather, a person must comply with the particulars of the divine law in order to qualify as a "true" believer. The puritan trend is thus uncompromising in its rejection of all forms of belief and ritual that do not qualify as the "true" religion of God.

As to the principles that should guide the interaction between Muslims and non-Muslims, the puritan trend cites the Qur'anic verse commanding Muslims to fight the unbelievers, "until there is no more tumult or oppression, and until faith and all judgment belongs to God."[4] Moreover, justifying an essentially supremacist view towards non-Muslims, proponents of puritanism often quote the following Qur'anic injunction: "Fight those among the People of the Book (Jews and Christians) who do not believe in God or the Hereafter, who do not forbid what God and His Prophet have forbidden, and who do not acknowledge the religion of truth—fight them until they pay the poll tax (*jizyah*) with willing submission and feel themselves subdued."[5]

Relying on such textual evidence, Muslim puritans assert that Muslims are the inheritors of an objectively ascertainable and realizable divine truth; while Jews and Christians may be tolerated, they cannot be befriended. Ultimately, however, they must be subdued and forced to acknowledge Muslim supremacy by paying a poll tax. The puritan doctrine is not necessarily or entirely dismissive of the rights of non-Muslims, and it does not necessarily lead to the persecution of Jews and Christians. But it does assert a hierarchy of importance, and the commitment to toleration is correspondingly fragile and contingent. So it is conducive to an arrogance that can easily descend into a lack of respect or concern for the well-being or dignity of non-Muslims. When this arrogant orientation is coupled with textual sources that exhort Muslims to fight against unbelievers (*kuffar*), it can produce a radical belligerency.

THE CASE FOR TOLERANCE IN ISLAM

The puritans construct their exclusionary and intolerant theology by reading Qur'anic verses in isolation, as if the meaning of the verses were transparent—as if moral ideas and historical context were irrelevant to their interpretation. In fact, however, it is impossible to analyze these and other verses except in light of the overall moral thrust of the Qur'anic message. The Qur'an itself refers to general moral imperatives such as mercy, justice, kindness, or goodness. The Qur'an does not clearly define any of these categories, but presumes a certain amount of moral probity on part of the reader. For instance, the Qur'an persistently commands Muslims enjoin the good. The word used for "the good" is *ma'ruf,* which means that which is commonly known to be good. Goodness, in the Qur'anic discourse, is part of what one may call a lived reality—it is the product of human experience, and constructed normative understandings. Similarly, the Qur'anic term for kindness is *ihsan,* which literally means to beautify and improve upon. But beautification or improving upon can have meaning only in the context of a certain sociological understanding and practice. In a further example, as to justice, the Qur'an states: "O you who believe, stand firmly for justice, as witnesses for God, even if it means testifying against yourselves, or your parents, or your kin, and whether it is against the rich or poor, for God prevails upon all. Follow not the lusts of your hearts, lest you swerve, and if you distort justice or decline to do justice, verily God knows what you do."[6] The idea that Muslims must stand up for justice even against their own self-interests is predicated on the notion that human beings are capable of achieving a high level of moral agency. As agents, Muslims are expected to achieve a level of moral conscientiousness, which they will bring to their relationship with God. In regards to every ethical obligation, the Qur'anic text assumes that readers will bring a preexisting, innate moral sense to the text. Hence, the text will morally enrich the reader, but only if the reader will morally enrich the text. The meaning of the religious text is not fixed simply by the literal meaning of its words, but depends, too, on the moral construction given to it by the reader. So if the reader approaches the text without moral commitments, it will almost inevitably yield nothing but discrete, legalistic, technical insights.

Similarly, it is imperative to analyze the historical circumstances in which specific Qur'anic ethical norms were negotiated. Many of the institutions referenced in the Qur'an—such as the poll tax or the formation of alliances with non-Muslims—can be understood only if the reader is aware of the historical practices surrounding the revelation of the text. But by emptying the Qur'an both of its historical and moral context, the puritan trend ends up transforming the text into a long list of morally noncommittal legal commands.

The Qur'anic discourse, for instance, can readily support an ethic of diversity and tolerance. The Qur'an not only expects, but even accepts the reality of difference and diversity within human society: "O humankind, God has created you from male and female and made you into diverse nations and tribes so that you may come to know each other. Verily, the most honored of you in the sight of God is he who is the most righteous."[7] Elsewhere, the Qur'an asserts that diversity is part of the divine intent and purpose in creation: "If thy Lord had willed, He would have made humankind into a single nation, but they will not cease to be diverse. . . . And, for this God created them [humankind]."[8] The classical commentators on the Qur'an did not fully explore the implications of this sanctioning of diversity, or the role of peaceful conflict resolution in perpetuating the type of social interaction that would result in people "knowing each other." Nor does the Qur'an provide specific rules or instructions about how "diverse nations and tribes" are to acquire such knowledge. In fact, the existence of diversity as a primary purpose of creation, as suggested by the verse above, remained underdeveloped in Islamic theology. Premodern Muslim scholars did not have a strong incentive to explore the meaning and implications of the Qur'anic endorsement of diversity and cross-cultural intercourse. This is partly because of the political dominance and superiority of the Islamic civilization, which left Muslim scholars with a sense of self-sufficient confidence. Nevertheless, it is fair to say that the Islamic civilization was pluralistic and unusually tolerant of various social and religious denominations. Working out the implications of a commitment to human diversity and mutual knowledge under contemporary conditions requires moral reflection and attention to historical circumstance—precisely what is missing from puritan theology and doctrine.

Other than a general endorsement of human diversity,

the Qur'an also accepted the more specific notion of a plurality of religious beliefs and laws. Although the Qur'an clearly claims that Islam is the divine truth, and demands belief in Muhammad as the final messenger in a long line of Abrahamic prophets, it does not completely exclude the possibility that there might be other paths to salvation. The Qur'an insists on God's unfettered discretion to accept in His mercy whomever He wishes. In a rather remarkable set of passages that, again, have not been adequately theorized by Muslim theologians, the Qur'an recognizes the legitimate multiplicity of religious convictions and laws. In one such passage, for example, the Qur'an asserts: "To each of you God has prescribed a Law and a Way. If God would have willed, He would have made you a single people. But God's purpose is to test you in what he has given each of you, so strive in the pursuit of virtue, and know that you will all return to God [in the Hereafter], and He will resolve all the matters in which you disagree."[9] On this and other occasions the Qur'an goes on to state that it is possible for non-Muslims to attain the blessing of salvation.: "Those who believe, those who follow Jewish scriptures, the Christians, the Sabians, and any who believe in God and the Final Day, and do good, all shall have their reward with their Lord and they will not come to fear or grief."[10] Significantly, this passage occurs in the same chapter that instructs Muslims not to take the Jews and Christians as allies. How can these different verses be reconciled?

If we read the text with moral and historical guidance, we

can see the different passages as part of a complex and layered discourse about reciprocity and its implications in the historical situation in Muhammad's Medina. In part, the chapter exhorts Muslims to support the newly established Muslim community in Medina. But its point is not to issue a blanket condemnation against Jews and Christians (who "shall have their reward with their Lord"). Instead, it accepts the distinctiveness of the Jewish and Christian communities and their laws, while also insisting that Muslims are entitled to the same treatment as those other communities. Thus it sets out an expectation of reciprocity for Muslims: while calling upon Muslims to support the Prophet of Islam against his Jewish and Christian detractors, it also recognizes the moral worth and rights of the non-Muslim "other."

The challenge most often invoked against an argument for tolerance in Islam is the issue of jihad. Jihad, especially as portrayed in the Western media, is often associated with the idea of a holy war that is propagated in the name of God against the unbelievers. Therefore, jihad is often equated with the most vulgar images of religious intolerance.

At the most rudimentary level, the Qur'an itself is explicit in prohibiting any form of coerced conversions to Islam. It contends that truth and falsity are clear and distinct, and so whomever wishes to believe may do so, but no duress is permitted in religion: "There is no compulsion in matter of faith."[11] Of course, this response is incomplete—even if forced conversions to Islam are prohibited, aggressive warfare to spread Islamic power over nonbelievers might still be allowed. Does the Qur'an condone such expansionist wars?

Interestingly, Islamic tradition does not have a notion of holy war. Jihad simply means to strive hard or struggle in pursuit of a just cause, and according to the Prophet of Islam, the highest form of jihad is the struggle waged to cleanse oneself from the vices of the heart. Holy war (*al-harb al-muqaddasah*) is not an expression used by the Qur'anic text or Muslim theologians. In Islamic theology, war is never holy; it is either justified or not, and if it is justified, those killed in battle are considered martyrs. The Qur'anic text does not recognize the idea of unlimited warfare, and does not consider the simple fact of the belligerent's Muslim identity to be sufficient to establish the justness of his cause. In other words, the Qur'an entertains the possibility that the Muslim combatant might be the unjust party in a conflict.

Moreover, while the Qur'an emphasizes that Muslims may fight those who fight them, it also insists that Muslims may not transgress.[12] Transgression is an ambiguous term, but on several occasions the Qur'an intimates that in order not to transgress, Muslims must be constrained by a requirement of proportionality, even when the cause is just. For instance, it states, "Mandated is the law of equality, so that who transgresses against you, respond in kind, and fear God, and know that God is with those who exercise restraint."[13]

Despite the prohibition against transgression and the

condemnation of unlimited warfare, many classical jurists adopted an imperialist orientation, which divided the world into the abode of Islam and the abode of war, and supported expansionist wars against unbelievers. But this view was not unanimous. Classical Muslim jurists debated whether unbelief is a sufficient justification for warfare, with a sizeable number of classical jurists arguing that non-Muslims may not be fought unless they pose a physical threat to Muslims. If non-Muslims seek peace, Muslims should make an effort to achieve such a peace. This discourse was partly inspired by the Qur'anic injunctions concerning peace. The Qur'an asserts that God does not prohibit Muslims from making peace with those who do not fight Muslims, but God does prohibit Muslims from making peace with those who have expelled Muslims from their homes and continue to persecute them.[14] Elsewhere, the Qur'an pronounces a stronger mandate in favor of peace in stating: "If your enemy inclines towards peace, then you should seek peace and trust in God."[15] Moreover, the Qur'an instructs Muslims not to haughtily turn away unbelievers who seek to make peace with Muslims, and reminds Muslims, "If God would have willed, He would have given the unbelievers power over you [Muslims], and they would have fought you [Muslims]. Therefore, if they [the unbelievers] withdraw from you and refuse to fight you, and instead send you guarantees of peace, know that God has not given you a license [to fight them]."[16] These discussions of peace would not make sense if Muslims were in a permanent state of war with nonbelievers, and if nonbelievers were a permanent enemy and always a legitimate target.

The other major issue on the point of tolerance in Islam is that of the poll tax (*jizyah*) imposed on the People of the Book (Christians and Jews) who live in Muslim territory. When the Qur'an was revealed, it was common inside and outside of Arabia to levy poll taxes against alien groups. Building upon the historical practice, classical Muslim jurists argued that the poll tax is money collected by the Islamic polity from non-Muslims in return for the protection of the Muslim state. If the Muslim state was incapable of extending such protection to non-Muslims, it was not supposed to levy a poll tax. In fact, 'Umar (r. 13–23/634–44), the second Rightly-Guided Caliph and close companion of the Prophet, returned the poll tax to an Arab Christian tribe that he was incapable of protecting from Byzantine aggression.

Aside from the juristic theory justifying the poll tax, the Qur'an does not, however, pronounce an absolute and unwavering rule in favor of such an institution. Once more, attention to historical circumstance is essential. The Qur'an endorsed a poll tax as a response to particular groups in Arabia who were persistently hostile to the early Muslims. Importantly, the Prophet did not collect a poll tax from every non-Muslim tribe that submitted to Muslim sovereignty, and in fact, in the case of a large number of non-Muslim but non-hostile tribes, he paid them a periodic sum of money or goods. These tribes were known as "those whose hearts have been reconciled." Furthermore, 'Umar entered into a peace settlement with Arab Christian tribes pursuant to which these tribes were obligated to pay the Islamic annual tax known as the *zakah* (almsgiving), and not the poll tax. Reportedly, although they refused to convert to Islam, the Christian tribes contended that paying the *jizyah* was degrading, and instead, asked to the pay the *zakah,* and 'Umar accommodated their request.[17] In short, there are various indicators that the poll tax is not a theologically mandated practice, but a functional solution that was adopted in response to a specific set of historical circumstances. Only an entirely ahistorical reading of the text could conclude that it is an essential element in a divinely sanctioned program of subordinating the nonbeliever.

Final Thoughts

Ultimately, the Qur'an, or any text, speaks through its reader. This ability of human beings to interpret texts is both a blessing and a burden. It is a blessing because it provides us with the flexibility to adapt texts to changing circumstances. It is a burden because the reader must take responsibility for the normative values he or she brings to the text. Any text, including those that are Islamic, provides possibilities for meaning, not inevitabilities. And those possibilities are exploited, developed and ultimately determined by the reader's efforts—good faith efforts, we hope—at making sense of the text's complexities. Consequently, the meaning of the text is often only as moral as its reader. If the reader is intolerant, hateful, or oppressive, so will be the interpretation of the text.

It would be disingenuous to deny that the Qur'an and other Islamic sources offer possibilities of intolerant interpretation. Clearly these possibilities are exploited by the contemporary puritans and supremacists. But the text does not command such intolerant readings. Historically, Islamic civilization has displayed a remarkable ability to recognize possibilities of tolerance, and to act upon these possibilities. Islamic civilization produced a moral and humanistic tradition that preserved Greek philosophy, and generated much science, art, and socially benevolent thought. Unfortunately, however, the modern puritans are dissipating and wasting this inspiring moral tradition. They are increasingly shutting off the possibilities for a tolerant interpretation of the Islamic tradition.

If we assess the moral trajectory of a civilization in light of its past record, then we have ample reason to be optimistic about the future. But the burden and blessing of sustaining that moral trajectory—of accentuating the Qur'anic message of tolerance and openness to the other—falls squarely on the shoulders of contemporary Muslim interpreters of the tradition.

2

PURITANISM AND STAGNATION

MILTON VIORST

September 11, as Khaled Abou El Fadl points out, has focused world attention on interpretation of the Qur'an, particularly on the extreme views taken by terrorists. In his
brilliant essay, he has gone far beyond the clichés that well-
meaning Western experts and Muslim clergy have employed to refute them. He has given us chapter and verse, so
to speak, of an alternate perception, of a humanist Islam,
and he makes a persuasive theological case for its legitimacy.
My reservation—recognizing it as a step removed from his
goal—is that in examining how terrorists have exploited the
Qur'an, he has overlooked the impact that interpretation
has had on Islamic society as a whole.

My conviction is that *conventional* interpretation—not
far different from that of the terrorists but without the justification of violence—must be held accountable for the economic and political stagnation that pervades Muslim society today. I do not blame Islam itself, which, as Abou El
Fadl justly notes, can be read in many ways. But *conventional*
interpretation—that which guides the conduct of most
Muslims—serves to suppress individual creativity and in-
novation. It has transformed a culture whose brilliance
once dazzled the world into a social backwater. In an age of

{ 27 }

rising global prosperity, it has placed Muslims on the brink of becoming a permanent global underclass.

Abou El Fadl, without emphasizing its scope, nonetheless attributes the problem to the rise of Wahhabism in the eighteenth century and its rebirth under the Saudi king 'Abd al-'Aziz at the beginning of the twentieth. The Saudis, he argues, have committed much of the fortune they later acquired from oil to spreading the doctrine, thereby nourishing an intellectual paralysis in Islamic culture. While devoting its energies to crushing the fruits of Marxism, the West ignored Wahhabism's offspring, notably Osama bin Laden and his ilk. To be fair, the Saudis did not foresee the savage predilections of these offspring, either. But Abou El Fadl is correct in citing their responsibility for spreading a doctrine—he prefers "puritanism" to "fundamentalism"—that promoted Muslim decline.

Abou El Fadl does not mention, however, (perhaps for reasons of space) that Islam's rejection of humanist values in favor of otherworldliness long predated the Saudis. The decision was made under the Abbasids during the golden age of Arab civilization, a thousand years before. The Abbisid caliphs entertained a school of Islamic scholars called Mu'tazilites who had been profoundly influenced by the wisdom of ancient Greece, which they encountered in documents acquired over the course of the Arab conquests. On the basis of these documents, they urged Muslims to transform the austere, legalistic faith that had reached them from the desert into a humane religion based on reason. Defending traditional Islam were the *ulama*, its leading jurists, who in fierce battle prevailed not just over the Mu'tazilites but over the caliphate itself. Their triumph left Mu'tazilite ideas to the recesses of Islamic history.

It is an irony of this history that what the Muslims called "Greek wisdom," the Mu'tazalite heritage, passed on to the West, where it gave birth to the Renaissance. Under this influence, the West humanized its values, while in Islam, scholars imbued with "a sense of self-sufficient confidence," as Abou El Fadl puts it, rejected "diversity and cross-cultural intercourse." With no experience comparable to the Renaissance, which was to give the West the Enlightenment and then the Scientific Revolution, the Islamic world continued on its inward journey. Even when a "modernist" Islam appeared under the influence of colonialism a century ago, Wahhabism seized upon its invitation to explore the roots of the faith (Salafism) to justify its own deepening puritanism. The open, tolerant Islam that Abou El Fadl finds in the Qur'an never acquired a place in the hearts of believers.

Abou El Fadl concludes his essay with the observation that "Ultimately the Qur'an, or any text, speaks through its readers." He is correct, of course. Jews and Christians are as disposed as Muslims to make of their scriptures whatever they want. What he does not say is that the reader, whatever faith he practices, is rarely an individual who imparts a personal meaning to the text. Far more commonly, the texts speak through those who command them. Great wars of religion have been fought over whose reading a society is to accept as authentic. For better or worse, Islamic texts are today ruled by jurists who give them puritan meanings, who discourage reinterpretation, who use them to preserve the intellectual and political status quo. These jurists safeguard the values and practices that keep Islamic society from changing with the times, that preserve its weakness in an increasingly dynamic world.

In offering us an insightful departure from the wisdom of these jurists, Abou El Fadl makes clear that Muslims, keeping the faith, have choices. His work will be studied with interest in the outside world, where—not coincidentally—he lives and works. In the Muslim world, he is likely to be ignored, if not vilified, for his efforts. Indeed, the elites of Islamic society are harsh with those who raise doubts about the foundations of their power. Most of these elites simply reject such ideas as are conveyed by Abou El Fadl and others who wish the Islamic world well. These ideas, alas, make it clear that the problems that Muslim society faces today, whether the focus is on terrorism or economic stagnation, are largely brought on by Muslims themselves.

A CONSERVATIVE LEGACY

SOHAIL H. HASHMI

I have long been intrigued by an exchange between Abraham and God that comes early in the Qur'an: "Behold! Abraham said: 'My lord! Show me how you give life to the dead.' [God] said: 'Do you not then have faith?' He said: 'Yes, but [I ask this] to satisfy my heart.' [God] replied: 'Take then four birds and teach them to incline toward [or obey] you. Then place a part of them on every hill around you, and then summon them. They will come flying to you. And know that God is almighty, wise'" (2:260). This verse follows several others and precedes many more in which Abraham is depicted as steadfast in his private faith and his public preaching—so much so that he is called *khalil Allah* (the friend of God) based on Q. 4:125. Why would the Qur'an even allude, I have wondered, to the possibility that this great prophet of God would harbor any doubts about God's power? Could it be that through this dialogue the Qur'an is intimating that skepticism and open questioning are intrinsic aspects of faith?

To me, this verse is one of the most powerful commandments for tolerance contained in the Qur'an, for if God can answer a prophet's troubled heart with such compassionate understanding, how much more likely is He to understand the doubts of ordinary humans? And if God understands, then how much more incumbent is it upon us human beings to do the same?

The Qur'an is a deep well from which Muslims may draw plentiful supplies of tolerance, pluralism, respect for diversity—even doubt. Khaled Abou El Fadl outlines these resources well in his thoughtful essay. I agree with him that such resources have been misappropriated by Muslim puritans and extremists. But his argument for misappropriation fails to account for the more widespread exclusivity and intolerance that we encounter in the Islamic intellectual heritage. Narrow and illiberal readings of the Qur'an are not exclusively the province of fringe elements. If that were so, the task of constructing liberal and tolerant societies among Muslim populations would be immeasurably easier. If contemporary Muslims are to realize the full "blessings" of the Qur'an's spirit, as Abou El Fadl urges, they must face up to the full "burden" of their political and intellectual history.

I want to be clear about my argument: I am not suggesting that Islamic history is one of intolerance. The historical record is clear that Islamic societies of the pre-modern period were generally as accommodating of diversity and religious freedom as their contemporaries in other parts of the world, and in many instances more so. The same cannot be said of modern Islamic states and societies, which lag far behind international standards of equality, democracy, and human rights. My point is that whether we are discussing tolerance, diversity, and freedom in pre-modern or modern

Islamic societies, Muslims have generally fallen far short of *Qur'anic standards*. And some of the responsibility for this failure in practice must be ascribed to the limitations in the interpretation of the Qur'an itself.

To return to Q. 2:260, for example: The most influential commentators have gone to great lengths to eliminate the faintest hint of doubt from Abraham's plea to God. Most classical and modern exegetes agree with al-Qurtubi (d. 1273) that Abraham's request does not signify doubt at all, only the desire "to rise from the knowledge of certainty [*'ilm al-yaqin*] to the reality of certainty [*'ayn al-yaqin*]."[1] Underlying this exegetical activity is the orthodox dogma that prophets are protected from error and doubt. This principle has to be maintained even if it requires glossing over God's direct question to Abraham, "Do you not then have faith?" If God were to give Abraham "the reality of certainty," then Abraham would no longer require faith. Moreover, we ordinary humans cannot likewise petition God for proof to solidify our faith.

The Qur'an repeatedly points to the complexities and ambiguities of faith. It stresses throughout the narrow line separating righteousness from self-righteousness, and admonishes believers to be humble in the knowledge that no person or even any creed can claim to have the full truth. Yet repeatedly, the tradition of Qur'anic exegesis strains to prove the opposite.

Let us consider how two Qur'anic verses cited by Abou El Fadl have been treated over the long history of exegesis.

First, Q. 2:62: "Those who believe, and the Jews, the Christians, and the Sabians—any who believe in God and the Last Day, and act righteously shall have their reward with their Lord. On them shall be no fear, nor shall they grieve." The verse seems clearly to be extending God's salvation to all humans who profess faith and do good deeds. Nevertheless, the majority of classical commentators found ways to limit its promise. One method was to argue for what Jane McAuliffe calls "salvific stages": thus only Jews, Christians, and Sabians who had adhered to the "pristine" faith—which Islamic belief holds to be common to all prophets—*before* the advent of Islam are promised God's favor in the afterlife.[2] Once Muhammad brought the final revelation, only true Muslims should consider this verse as applying to them.

A second means of circumscribing the verse's universality, which reinforces the first, is to argue that it has been abrogated by subsequent revelation, including Q. 3:85: "If anyone desires a religion other than Islam, never will it be accepted of him, and in the hereafter he will be among the losers." Instead of attempting to reconcile the verses by contextualizing them in time and in the full Qur'anic text, many exegetes have employed the principle of abrogation as a blunt instrument. Hundreds of verses could, in this manner, be labeled "no longer relevant." The fact that Q. 2:62 is repeated almost verbatim in Q. 5:69, a verse believed to have been revealed after Q. 3:85, is conveniently forgotten.

Q. 2:62's message of tolerance is indirect; Muslims have

no monopoly in the life to come and thus can claim no exclusive righteousness in this life. Another verse cited by Abou El Fadl, Q. 5:48, far more directly asserts that religious diversity is not something simply to be tolerated as a necessary evil, but a necessary good to be embraced by all who sincerely strive for the truth: "To each among you have We prescribed a law and an open path. If God had so willed, He would have made you one community. But [His plan is] to test you in what He has given you. So strive as in a race in all the virtues. The goal of you all is to God. It is He who will show you the truth of the matters in which you differ."

This verse is so arresting in its breadth, clarity, and self-confidence that it would seem to leave little room for controversy. Yet again, mainstream Qur'anic interpreters found ways to problematize the clearest verses, whose meaning is buttressed by the thrust of Qur'anic teaching, while upholding other verses of limited scope as authoritative. Thus, Ibn Kathir (d. 1373)—following a line of reasoning developed by al-Tabari (d. 923) and others—suggests that the separate communities addressed in this verse are pre-Muhammadan communities, and that with the advent of the Muslim community, all other previously valid courses had been annulled by Islam.[3] The fact that the verse contains the imperative verb *istabiqu,* which conveys the sense of multiple, contemporaneous actors "vying" or "racing" toward virtue, is again conveniently glossed over.

There are of course a number of political and sociological reasons why the exegetical tradition tended toward conservatism and exclusivity when dealing with Qur'anic views of the other. These historical factors need not detain us here; what is most important is to acknowledge this legacy frankly and to chart a course that both responds to it and departs from it. Contemporary Muslim interpreters can ill afford to disregard the conservative legacy, or simply associate it with extremist forms of Islam, for the Qur'an still speaks to millions of the faithful through the voices of its classical commentators. But if modern Muslims are to build tolerant and pluralistic societies based on Qur'anic teachings, they must also be prepared to chart a new exegetical course.

THEOLOGICAL DISTRACTIONS

TARIQ ALI

Although I agree with much that Khaled Abou El Fadl says in his discussion of Islam and toleration, I fundamentally disagree with his emphasis on theological issues to explain the actions of people and societies. I will concentrate here on the problems that arise when the questions raised by September 11 are dealt with exclusively through the prism of Muslim theology. Priests and ministers have often provided divine sanction for wars, colonization, and imperial missions. Rabbis and mullahs are no different. Nor are their followers. The fanatical Jewish settlers in Palestinian lands and the followers of al-Qaeda have much in common. Comparative histories of the three monotheisms are far more useful in this regard than theology. The points below are designed to clarify the debate:

(1) The fact that the attacks of September 11 were carried out under the cloak of religion should not obscure the underlying issues. The Old Testament and the Qur'an are open to many interpretations. All factions can drink from these wells and this makes them powerful as ideologies. It is true that at various times in Islamic history, religious scholars achieved a relative degree of autonomy from political

power, but ultimately the *qadi*'s choice was limited: to bow before the Sultan or the executioner. In fact this tension was present in Islam from the very beginning. Muhammad was not in favor of a clergy on the Christian model. The Caliph was both the temporal and the spiritual ruler. A clergy did develop, in part because the rapid growth of Islam necessitated a religious bureaucracy that could pronounce the verdict of Islam on new problems each week. The Qur'an was used as a reference, but traditions had to be invented to facilitate Muslim rule in different parts of the world. As with the Talmud, rival Muslim scholars in the pay of rival rulers or factions could interpret a Qur'anic verse in different ways. I see no point debating with Islamic puritans on whose interpretation is correct. To do so is to fight the war on their battlefield.

The real question is why bin Laden and his gang turned against their former patrons. The answer has very little to do with religion, but a great deal to do with history and politics. Because the causes are political, not religious, the solution has to be political, not military or civilizational. If, as Fukuyama has argued, the members of al-Qaeda are "Islamo-fascists," then one has to ask: when did they become Islamo-fascists? Their religious views have not altered since the time they were recruited by the United States, Saudi Arabia, and Egypt for the "jihad" against the Soviets in Afghanistan. Were they Islamo-fascists when President Carter's envoy, Zbigniew Brzezinski, stood on the Pak-Afghan border and told the bearded assembly: "God is on your side," or did the transformation take place after September 11?

The basic fact is that radical Islam was brought into being by the needs of the Cold War. The irony is that the Wahhabi state in Saudi Arabia, the most conservative social formation in the Islamic world, became the conduit for funding and arming radical Islamists all over the world with full approval from Washington.

(2) State control in Islamic countries over once-autonomous religious endowments is hardly surprising. Muslim societies were subjected to the storms of the twentieth century, just like every other part of the world. Kemal Ataturk in Turkey was the first to separate religion from the state and abolish the Caliphate after the First World War. Egypt, Syria, and Iraq were ruled by radical-nationalist secular regimes in the late fifties and sixties. The defeat of Arab nationalism by a U.S.-backed Israel in 1967 created a big vacuum in the region. The staunchly secular Baath Party has been in power in Syria and Iraq for nearly half a century. In Egypt, Anwar Sadat brought the Islamists into the center of politics by hurling them into battle against the nationalists and communists. Then he cut a deal with Israel and his Islamist friends killed him: the first blowback. In Algeria, the French encouraged the FLN leadership to sideline the radicals by encouraging the formation of the FIS. This, too, became a Frankenstein's monster.

So wherever we look, it becomes clear that the Qur'an is not the problem, but the interests of various Western states are. Even after September 11, Tony Blair grins like a disc jockey and encourages the development of more single-faith schools in Britain, a country where a large majority (unlike the United States) does not believe in a deity.

(3) To search for a post-modern identity politics using the resources of Islam is a futile exercise. The Islamic world needs a reformation to develop ideas on every level—philosophical, political, economic—that take it beyond the past in which it has mired itself and beyond the neoliberal orthodoxy on offer from the West. This reformation will require a rigid separation of state and mosque; thoroughgoing democratization of the Islamic world including Saudi Arabia, Kuwait, and Egypt. If Christian Democratic parties can function in Western Europe, then Islamic-Democratic parties can function in Egypt, Turkey, or Algeria. Above all, intellectuals in the Muslim world must assert their right to interpret texts that are the collective property of Islamic culture as a whole. Islam's traditions of intellectual inquiry tragically atrophied after its first few centuries. There was more dissent and skepticism in Islam during the eleventh and twelfth centuries than there is today. In reality millions of skeptics, agnostics, and atheists currently live in the Islamic world. They dare not speak in public for fear of the response, but they will not keep silent forever.

* * *

(4) Interestingly, the country that might witness the most dramatic reformation is Iran. The bulk of the Iranian population is under thirty-five and their religious and political experiences have been primarily shaped by clerical despotism. Mercifully the United States has not intervened and confused matters. So the development of the burgeoning anticlerical movement in Iran is organic. Young people of both sexes taunt and challenge the religious police, which guards orthodoxy. Hatred of religion and the clergy is growing underneath the surface. Voices within the clergy itself are promising reform. It is still early to predict the exact shape of Iran's future, but change there could impact every state in the house of Islam. In other words the story is not yet over. We need to move beyond discussing whether or not the Qur'an promotes tolerance and grapple with the urgent social and political problems that affect the Muslim world.

The flow of recruits to such groups as al-Qaeda will be stemmed neither by advancing a different view of Islam through Qur'anic interpretation nor by the so-called "War on Terror." The latter actually only aggravates widespread despair and will produce future violence. The situation demands political solutions: Israel/Palestine and Iraq are the issues that lead young middle-class, university-educated professionals in the direction of terrorism. It is urgent that the "international community" address their anxieties, which are based on real problems. Theology in this regard is useless.

THE LIMITS OF TOLERANCE

ABID ULLAH JAN

Since September 11, Islamic teachings and Muslims have been blamed for every variety of terrorism, intolerance, and extremism in the world. The long-term anti-Islam campaign, once spearheaded by a few American analysts, has suddenly become mainstream and many Muslims have proudly joined the ranks of the critics. Gone is the search for real evidence and culprits in the events of September 11. At the top of the agenda now is the place of tolerance in Islam and compatibility of this faith with the contemporary world.

Opportunist Muslim opinion-makers are leading the pack of so-called moderate intellectuals who pretend to bridge the ever-widening gap between Islam and the West. Khaled Abou El Fadl, for instance, wants Muslims to interpret the Qur'an in the context of ancient historical facts, but at the same time presents terrorism as an isolated phenomenon, independent of historical or political context. The cacophony of voices in the Western media presents just one reason for the troubles around the world: Islam.

According to Abou El Fadl, intolerant Muslims think that Islam is "the only way of life," and that it "must be pursued regardless of its impact on the rights and well-being of others." Ignoring U.S. efforts to impose its way of life on others, these analysts complain that Muslim "puritans" are "not satisfied with living according to their own dictates," but "aggressively seek to disempower, dominate, or destroy others." Closer analysis of the facts, however, reveals just how many global crises have a different source: in efforts by the United States and its allies to achieve economic and cultural hegemony by dominating or destroying all opposition. The words that Abou El Fadl uses—control, dominate, and destroy—are really more appropriate to Pat Robertson's recent efforts to demonize Islam through his media empire —which is rarely described as belonging to a "supremacist Christian."

When he seeks to assign responsibility for intolerance, Abou El Fadl should look no further than the Western quest for dominance. Did supremacist Muslim "puritans" initiate the troubles in Algeria? Are the Muslim "fundamentalists" occupying non-Muslim lands? Have they driven out more than 800,000 non-Muslims from their homes? Are the Muslim "extremists" killing people with a different way of life in Kashmir and Chechnya? Do "supremacist Muslims" dominate the United Nations and define rights and rules for the rest of the world to follow? Dictating secularized, liberalized, Western ways of life—isn't that "aggressively seeking to dominate others"? Imposing sanctions on Iraq, Iran, Libya, Sudan, Pakistan, Afghanistan—isn't that "disempowering others"? And what does "destroying others" mean if not the scale of destruction in the Gulf War and the sanctions that followed it?

We are now witnessing the second phase of an organized attempt to eliminate Islam. The first phase was launched in the early and mid-twentieth century, and the present state of virtual anarchy in the Muslim world is the direct result of that colonial aggression. The colonizers made a determined effort to end *khilafa,* centralize and empower the Muslim states, control the private religious endowments (*awqaf*) that once sustained the juristic class, co-opt the clergy, and transform them into salaried employees. This generated confusion about the true voice of religious authority. In the first phase, the clergy's legitimacy was targeted. Now, its very existence is being challenged. Religious groups are banned, madrassa are being transformed into nothing more than secular public schools, and words such as *mulla, maoulana, ulama, jihad,* and even *Islam* are being stigmatized. The profound vacuum in religious authority is being filled by revisionist interpreters of Islam like Abou El Fadl. It's easy to say that "militant Puritans" read Qur'anic verses "literally and ahistorically," but harder to substantiate such assertions. The Qur'an is not a simple book that anyone can interpret without the requisite knowledge and context; it is a guide for humanity and each verse is intended for the use of all generations to come until the day of judgment. It is thus facile and wrong to selectively dismiss certain passages as having no practical application today or to reject others as leading Muslims to "highly exclusionary conclusions."

As far the limits of tolerance are concerned, the frustration of Muslims around the world is not a consequence of faulty interpretations of Islam but of an inability to tolerate continued Western double standards and the treatment of Muslims as second-class citizens of the planet. And the Qur'an tells them explicitly in 4:135: "O you who believe, stand firmly for justice, as witnesses for Allah, even if it means testifying against yourselves, or your parents, or your kin, and whether it is against the rich or poor, for Allah prevails upon all. Follow not the lusts of your hearts, lest you swerve, and if you distort justice or decline to do justice, verily Allah knows what you do."

The supposed problem of Islamic "intolerance" is in fact principled resistance demonstrated by the Muslims who stand up for justice even against their own self-interests. The Taliban knew their military disadvantage against the coalition of Western powers, but they refused, on principle, to hand over a suspect without sufficient evidence. Indeed, it is ludicrous for Abou El Fadl to mourn for an historical Islamic civilization that "was pluralistic and unusually tolerant of various social and religious denominations," because Islam is still uncommonly tolerant of other peoples and religions. Why doesn't anyone talk about a crisis of tolerance in Judaism when dozens of the Palestinians have been killed on a weekly basis for the last thirty-five years? Why is the media silent about intolerant Hinduism that has relentlessly oppressed Kashmiri Muslims for the last fifty-five years? Why didn't the analysts speculate about intolerance in Christianity when 300,000 Muslims were butchered in Bosnia? And why not now, as Muslims face the wrath of Russians in Chechnya? Why are the lectures on tolerance directed at Islam alone? Simply because the victim of September 11 was the United States.

In an attempt to please Islam-bashers, Muslims like Abou El Fadl go to the extreme of arguing that Islam is but one of many paths to salvation. In support of their claim, they quote verses, such as 5:48 and 5:69, out of context and ignore the crux of Islamic belief system. For instance, the words *"Shara'a lakum mina alddeeni"* (He has ordained for you the same law) in 42:13 and *"likullin ja'alna minkum shir-AAatan waminhajan"* (to each of you we have prescribed a law and a clear way) in 5:48 do not justify Abou El Fadl's argument that Islam is but one road to salvation. We have to look at these verses in the context of three very distinct boundaries drawn by the Qur'an among *deen* (the overall belief system), *shari'a* (law/way) and *minhaj* (approach).

Deen is actually the belief that Allah is the *only* supreme ruler and His messengers are his representatives, like: "There is no God but Allah and Muhammad (PBUH) is his messenger." This way, names of the prophets would change, but the declaration would remain the same, which means Moses, Jesus, Noah, and Muhammad (PBUH) preached the same *deen*—Islam. So *deen* is one: only *shari'a* and *minhaj* are different.

Minhaj-i-Ibrahim, for instance, was establishing monotheist institutions. *Minhaj-i-Mosa* was working as a savior of the enslaved people. *Minhaj-i-Isa* was moral and spiritual uplift, whereas *minhaj-i-Mohammed* (PBUH) is invitation to *deen*; organizing and training people, and establishing an Islamic government.

The Qur'an clearly refers in numerous places to *the only* path to salvation. The basic requirement is not to follow any of the previous *shari'a,* which were nullified after revelation of the last *shari'a* to Prophet Muhammad (PBUH). The provision of verse 5:69, quoted by Abou El Fadl, is abrogated by verse 3:85, which states: "And whoever seeks a religion other than Islam, it will never be accepted of him, and in the Hereafter he will be one of the losers."[1]

Besides, the basic condition is to believe in Allah and the Hereafter, and at the same time it is a must to obey Allah and His Messenger. "O mankind! The Messenger has come to you in truth from Allah: believe in him: it is best for you."[2] "Those who deny Allah and His Messenger, and wish to separate Allah from His Messenger saying: 'We believe in some but reject others'" and wish to take a course midway. They are in truth Unbelievers and we have prepared for unbelievers a humiliating punishment."[3]

Undoubtedly, Qur'an accepts the distinctiveness of the Jewish and Christian communities and their laws, while also insisting that Muslims are entitled to the same rights and respect as those other peoples. But nowhere does it suggest that all faiths lead to salvation. Of course, it sets out an expectation of reciprocity for Muslims, but it does not allow them to also follow Jewish and Christian practice and belief. It definitely recognizes the moral worth and rights of the non-Muslims but does not relieve Muslims of their responsibility to stand for the rights of their oppressed brethren. What crime did the Palestinians, Kashmiris, Chechens, Iraqis, and others commit?

It is wrong to claim that the meaning of Qur'an "is often only as moral as its reader," which means if the reader is intolerant, so too will be the interpretation of the text. If the text of the Qur'an were so fluid that anyone could interpret it according to his interest, it would never have been so different from every other book, from the era of its revelation until the present. Abou El Fadl claims that the Qur'an and other Islamic sources "offer possibilities of intolerant interpretation." Actually, it depends on who is judging the interpretation. The clear injunction to fight an oppressor is always going to be considered an "intolerant interpretation" by an oppressor. And those who educate and motivate people to stand up and face oppression will always be seen by oppressors as "puritans and supremacists." Applications of the Qur'an to real life situations will continue to be condemned as intolerant when they make life harder for intolerant oppressors.

Although it does not command "intolerant readings,"

Qur'an does prohibit tolerating injustice and the repression of innocents. Historically, Islamic civilization has displayed, and continues to display, a remarkable capacity for tolerance. The Islamic world has witnessed the butchery of 300,000 Bosnian Muslims, who were prevented from defending themselves by a skewed Western arms embargo. They have witnessed the vengeful war against the Taliban—despite the absence of any shred of evidence about their involvement in the attacks of September 11. And we witness the ongoing war against the Palestinian people, perhaps the most visible display of Western double standards.

The "modern puritans" are not dissipating and wasting the inspiring moral tradition of Islam; instead, modern world leaders are taking advantage of Islamic tolerance to force Muslims into greater subservience. They must not only surrender their right to stand for their oppressed brothers and sisters but also the right to call for justice—because "tolerant" interpreters of Islam forbid it. Qur'anic interpretation only goes wrong, according to these critics, when it hurts the interest of the merciless and mighty oppressor. The burden of sustaining the limits of tolerance in Islam falls squarely on the shoulders of the giants who trample on the rights of Muslims (or sustain the rule of their oppressors).

Islamic resistance is a call to self-defense against an endless reign of terror and violence. Islam simply happens to be the religion of the oppressed and those fighting for their rights in the absence of all political options. Blaming them for misinterpretation and urging them to be even more tolerant of oppression is not the solution. Islamic teachings would likely be more tolerant today, if the laws that apply to the Iraqis were also applied to the Israelis; if the laws that apply to those who died in the World Trade Center were also applied to those who died in Afghanistan; and if the universal principles applied to Kuwait and East Timor were also applied to Palestine and Kashmir. Oppression forever begets intolerance. And sermons about tolerance should not be used to help the West treat Muslims as second-rate people forever.

TEXT AND CONTEXT

STANLEY KURTZ

Let us say that Khaled Abou El Fadl is correct when he says that the Qur'an's tradition of tolerance was inadequately theorized by later scholars—most likely because the superiority and dominance of Islamic civilization itself gave those scholars little incentive to explore the nature and necessity of toleration. Let us further stipulate, in agreement with Abou El Fadl, that the imperialist orientation adopted by most pre-modern Islamic scholarship was ill-supported by the Qur'an itself. What would all that tell us about the nature of religion in general, and of Islam in particular?

It would seem to say that in matters religious, the contents of sacred texts are frequently less important than the social and historical settings in which those texts are interpreted. Of course, that is the sort of remark liable to be made by a secular social scientist—someone standing outside of whatever religious tradition is under consideration. But the interesting thing here is that Abou El Fadl himself is calling on Muslims to bring the sensibilities of an historical sociologist to their reading of the Qur'an. That sort of approach may be popular at liberal divinity schools and departments of religion at American universities, but I wonder how much appeal it will hold for Middle Eastern Muslims.

Successful religious reformations may in fact reinterpret and adapt sacred texts to changed social circumstances, but they rarely see themselves as doing so. Abou El Fadl may rightly charge Wahhabi scholars with projecting their contemporary cultural conservatism back onto the Qur'an, but that is precisely the mark of a successful religious movement. To a degree, Abou El Fadl's liberal reinterpretation of the Qur'an engages in exactly that sort of back-projection—a hopeful sign! But Abou El Fadl's honesty, tolerance, and intellectual integrity extend to an acknowledgment that the Qur'an, after all, is a complex and indeterminate text, and one that offers a good deal of justification, even for the intolerant interpretations of his theological opponents. That is an admirably liberal thing to say, but I fear that the appeal of this sort of reform will be restricted to those who have already accepted modernity—chiefly assimilated and highly educated Muslims in the United States, as well as the relatively small number of highly modernized Muslims in the Middle East itself.

If it is true that sacred texts are often less important, in and of themselves, than the social context in which they are interpreted, what shall we say about the current social context? The great sociologist Max Weber understood religions to have distinctive possibilities for action built into their traditions. Those traditions, said Weber, are shaped less by texts than by dominant social groups and critical historical experiences. However multiplex a given tradition, Weber

believed that, in times of social crisis, a religion's character-
istic modes of action would be "switched on."

Abou El Fadl argues that the essential lesson taught by Islamic history is that extremist groups are eventually ejected
from mainstream Islam, and tamed in the process. It might
be more accurate to say that Islam is characterized by the
continual reappearance of such extremist groups in times of
social stress (whatever their eventual fate). The appearance
of these totalizing and extremist religious movements is
itself rooted in the broader Islamic tradition of aggressive
conquest and religious rule—a tradition drawn, to a degree,
from the Qur'an itself, but shaped as well by the later experience of Islamic empire to which Abou El Fadl refers.

I don't believe that the rise of contemporary Wahhabism
or the various terrorist groups is best explained as a function
of Saudi oil revenues, or even as a reaction to Middle Eastern despotism in the present and colonial intervention in the
past. The rise of an intolerant and extremist Muslim fundamentalism is rooted instead in massive population increases
and urban migration throughout the Middle East. Traditional rural society, with its bonds of family and kinship, has
partially reconstituted itself in the new urban environment.
Yet that traditional social system is also gravely threatened
by innovations such as education and modern employment,
as these apply to both women and men.

Abou El Fadl refers to problems caused by despotic and
effectively illegitimate Muslim governments of the modern

Middle East, but this situation is itself a contemporary transformation of the traditional separation between the state and society in the Muslim world. After the passing of the rightly-guided Caliphs, Islamic governments lost much of their religious legitimacy, and were often merely tolerated by a society whose traditional tribal structure essentially allowed it to be self-governing. That arrangement worked well when Islamic rulers could cobble together empires out of coalitions of tribes (and minority communities) that more or less ran themselves. But in a contemporary context, there is a continual tension between the still powerful traditional kinship system and the modernizing imperatives of centralized bureaucratic government.

A vicious circle has been established in the modern Middle East in which the strength of traditional kinship ties undercuts the functioning of a modern political economy; economic and political failure in turn reinforces a retreat into, and combative defense of, the traditional social system. This is the crisis that has pushed so many educated but unemployed Muslim men into the arms of the fundamentalists. The same challenge of modernity has spurred a turn to veiling and fundamentalism among women torn between their commitment to education and employment, on the one hand, and the need to uphold the reputation and social position of their families, on the other.

Only when this vicious cycle is broken and some greater reconciliation between tradition and modernity on the level of fundamental social practice occurs can an ideological reformation succeed. Of course, a radical separation between social and ideological change is untenable. But Abou El Fadl's liberal pluralism is geared to appeal to people who live the way Americans live—as individuals, relatively free of social and family obligation. That is not how most people live in the Muslim Middle East, and will likely not be the way they live, even after some modus vivendi is established between the traditional Muslim family and kinship structure and modernity. So we don't yet know what the real reformation will look like—or even if it will come at all. But the reformation of Islam will not be brought about by innovative textual interpretation so much as it will depend upon fundamental social change.

BEYOND INTERPRETATION

AMINA WADUD

I want to commend Khaled Abou El Fadl for his insightful assessment of the attacks on New York City and the Pentagon and especially for his parallel historicization of those events and the work of Qur'anic interpretation. The tendency to de-contextualize September 11—to treat it as a single random act of violence—has been challenged by Muslim thinkers, activists, and political analysts since September 12. Many have been condemned as apologists for the heinous act, as if understanding implies forgiveness.

What is unusual here, and what draws my interest to this particular discussion is Abou El Fadl's juxtaposition of the historical reading of political events with an interpretive imperative that calls for a similar historical reading of the Qur'an. Indeed, the absence of such an historical reading has provided, he argues, a partial catalyst for the intolerant, exclusivist and extremist rendition of Qur'anic meaning advanced by Muslim puritans, who proceed from that understanding to the most extreme Muslim practice and the perpetration of violent acts.

What Abou El Fadl does not point out is that such extremist interpretive modalities and their resulting social operations are equally destructive within Muslim society as they are in non-Muslim communities. Within Muslim communities women are the primary victims. My own research on Qur'anic interpretation and implementation focuses on gender and the ways that exclusionary textual readings marginalize women's full human agency within society. Not only are non-Muslims subjected to subhuman standards and victimized by violent acts, but Muslim women are as well, as an outcome of practices that stem from the authoritarian voice of puritanical interpretations.

In explaining the distinction between tolerant and intolerant readings of the Qur'an, Abou El Fadl emphasizes that "puritans construct their exclusionary and intolerant theology by reading Qur'anic verses in isolation, as if the meaning of the verses were transparent—as if moral ideas and historical context were irrelevant to their interpretation." In contrast he asserts that it is "impossible to analyze these and other verses except in light of the overall moral thrust of the Qur'anic message" for certain general moral imperatives that, while not clearly defined, presume "a certain amount of moral probity on [the] part of the reader." Thus, he continues, "the idea that Muslims must stand up for justice even against their own self-interests is predicated on the notion that human beings . . . achieve a level of moral conscientiousness, which they will bring to their relationship with God. . . . [T]he Qur'anic text assumes that readers will bring a pre-existing, innate moral sense to the text. Hence, the text will morally enrich the reader, but only if the reader will morally enrich the text."

I agree that interpretation demands interaction between the text and reader on several different levels: intellectual, spiritual, linguistic, and moral. But I would locate the higher level of this exchange not between the reader and the text but within the text itself as part of the divine origin of revelation. No matter how moral the reader is, he or she can only benefit maximally from this engagement with the text through surrender (*islam*) of the ego or of self-interest. Only then can the reader be witness to an unveiling of higher, deeper, and yet more subtle potentials of textual meaning for understanding and implementation.

This observation is fully consistent with Abou El Fadl's account of the mutual enrichment of text and reader. It merely states that religious belief, while ineffable and immeasurable, has a certain degree of significance to the enrichment that comes through reading. It presumes that the one who reads will be enriched more than the text being read. Furthermore, self-interest is a barrier to this enrichment of individual or collective reading and results, as Abou El Fadl puts it, in "emptying the Qur'an both of its historical and moral context . . . [and] transforming the text into a long list of morally non-committal legal commands."

Although textual meaning is not fixed, the actual utterances are immutable. Inevitably the reader has the greater flexibility and a greater potential for transformation than does the text. The Qur'an is an excellent catalyst in growth and transformation of moral consciousness but the manner of this enrichment remains part of the mystery of the divine becoming known through the text. These observations about interpretation lead to my strongest note of caution about Abou El Fadl's argument. He says both that "the Qur'anic discourse . . . can readily support an ethic of diversity and tolerance" and that it "would be disingenuous to deny that the Qur'an and other Islamic sources offer possibilities of intolerant interpretation . . . exploited by contemporary puritans and supremacists." But this observation simply returns to our starting place. We are no closer to determining precisely how to sustain the moral trajectory, and cannot expect that contemporary Muslim interpreters will carry the entire substantial burden.

Taking all of Abou El Fadl's insights into consideration, then, a more tenable proposal would be to enact a modern version of the "essential lesson taught by Islamic history . . . that extremist groups are ejected from the mainstream of Islam; they are marginalized, and eventually treated as heretical aberrations to the Islamic message." Along with contemporary liberatory interpretations of the text, this movement within the mainstream community would form a cohesive means of promoting the Qur'an's tolerant, inclusive message. What is needed, in short, is not simply an intellectual, interpretive enterprise (a less literal way to read the texts), but a deeply forged cooperation between intellectuals and lay Muslims—who after all number well over one billion and have been scrambling to reclaim the integrity of Islam from the acts committed by extremists, whose numbers cannot even amount to a fraction of a percent of their population. In other words, it is time for an historical moral imperative to come alive in contemporary Islam.

THE IMPORTANCE OF DEMOCRACY

AKEEL BILGRAMI

The absolutist (or what is sometimes called "fundamental-ist") conception of Islam bears a grotesque resemblance to the picture of Islam that is often presented by American journalists and academics. And when the latter start writing about the Qur'an as the basis of their understanding of Islam, the resemblance is even stronger because it is precisely the Qur'an that the fundamentalists invoke as inviolable testimony for their own position. In the aftermath of the events of last fall, these caricatures of Islam, coming (bizarrely) from two avowedly opposed directions, need more than ever to be addressed.

Khaled Abou El Fadl has written a worthy essay presenting the tolerant aspects of the Qur'an and the religion it announces. He does not conceal the handful of passages that have been constantly exploited by the fundamentalists, but he insists on embedding them in a broader moral and historical context in which they take on a significance markedly different from the absolutist interpretations. And he argues that the fundamentalists' crude and reductive vision of Islam as a fixed code of conduct cannot stand when confronted by such moral and historical readings.

First, he argues that the moral reading is demanded by

the text itself. Thus in Q. 4.135, justice is commended as the highest moral virtue. Abou El Fadl concludes that the Qur'an is in effect telling Muslims that they are to read the Qur'an with moral discrimination: in light of their sense of justice. If they do, then they will move beyond the literalist rendering of "discrete, legalistic, and technical insights" and find a message that is morally enriching and tolerant.

Second, the historical reading. Abou El Fadl's claim here is that there is no sensible way to understand the content of a number of Qur'anic revelations independent of the historical context in which they were given, and that once we understand them in this context, there is no further temptation to read them as a series of "morally noncommittal legal commands."

The moral argument is not, however, decisive. It by no means follows from the fact that the Qur'an exalts justice as primary among moral values that a tolerant Islam must be read into the Qur'an. What counts as "just" is notoriously contested, and it might as easily be claimed that the Qur'an's vision of justice is only realized by those who put aside their own moral predilections and adhere to the legalistic requirements of the literalist reading. In the passage that Abou El Fadl cites, justice is explicitly distinguished from self-interest. But that distinction does not rule out the literalist reading he opposes. After all, literalism does not elevate self-interest over moral virtue but of course accepts that self-interest is subservient to morality. What distinguishes literalism is that the content of morality is fixed by the literal understanding of the text.

Abou El Fadl's historical reading is both plausible and attractive but it is merely asserted here without argument, and is bound to be met with simple counter-assertions—both by absolutists who do not, on principle, accept any historical contextualization of the Qur'an, and by their Western critics who lack the sympathy necessary to accept such contextualization. To show that these are (respectively) unnecessarily dogmatic and uncharitable ways of reading the Qur'an, an *argument* will have to be found for Abou El Fadl's assertions. And it will help if the argument can appeal to elements *in the Qur'an itself* that help justify an historically contextual reading. There are two such identifiable elements.

First, there is the fact that the revelations contained in the Mecca verses are very different in character and content from the Medina verses. The former are almost exclusively restricted to the broad universalist and spiritualist aspects of the religion. The latter speak very specifically to matters of state, community, family, and interpersonal relations, including the relations that Muslims must bear to non-Muslims. And the latter contain most of the passages that the caricature of Islam exploits, in particular the passages that sanction gender injustice and hostile and aggressive relations with non-Muslims. So there is a textual justification for pointing out that the Medina verses were revealed in a very specific social and political context, different from that of the earlier Mecca verses, and still more different from those of contemporary societies both West and East. At Medina, the Prophet was in the position of having to carry a large, often faithless population toward the newly revealed faith—a highly nomadic population that could only achieve spiritual and practical stability through a sense of cultural *belonging*. That sense of belonging could only come if the faith itself spoke to questions of community, family, sexual and marital relations, and relations with communities of non-Muslim faiths that sometimes responded with hostility to the emerging faith.

The historical context of the Medina verses—a context of *conversion,* to put it in a word—having now lapsed, it is arguable that the *Mecca* verses should be stressed as the most significant governing ethos of the now entrenched faith. Such an argument need not take the form of a strident repudiation of the Medina revelations (and such a repudiation would be bound to make Muslim populations long-besieged by old and new forms of colonial subjugation feel even more defensive), but rather a gentle redirection of attention toward Islam's tolerant aspects emphasized in the earlier revelations. Abou El Fadl's essay admirably achieves just this tone and this reorientation.

A second element in the Qur'an that may help provide an argument for his historical reading is the contextualized place in the Qur'an of *earlier* prophets, prophecies, and peoples "of the book," which the Qur'an acknowledges as antecedents. The Qur'an presents Islam as historically superceding these faiths, but in doing so it implicitly acknowledges an idea and ideal of historical supercession and reinterpretation. Hence this idea and ideal cannot be dismissed dogmatically (as it is by uncritical fundamentalists) and uncharitably (as it is by their glib Western critics) as something alien to the spirit and content of the Qur'an.

My discussion thus far is meant to add argument in support of a reading of the Qur'an that is both necessary and admirably advanced by Abou El Fadl. But I feel it necessary to conclude by remarking on a more basic deficiency in his essay. Contemporary discussion of Islam and the Qur'an needs to be carried out with a full understanding that the real issue is only secondarily about a doctrine and a book, and primarily about Muslims as a people and their political life, a life that to a considerable extent is defined by a legacy of colonial rule that continues to this day in disguised and implicit forms that are well known, and denied only by insular Americans and (much more culpably) by intellectual mandarins in the media and universities.

Abou El Fadl himself is explicit about the fact that most Muslims are not fundamentalists and do not have a dogmatic or uncontextualized and literal reading of their book. But this fact raises an obvious question. If these are the overwhelming majority of Muslims, how is it that a much smaller group of Muslims who propagate a highly misleading caricature of Islam and its book gets to be the representative voice of Islam? The answer too is obvious. Whenever there is a democratic election, whether in Pakistan or in Iran, this minority of fundamentalists is shown up as just what it is: an *unrepresentative* group. The record of success of parties and leaders standing and speaking for such groups in Islamic nations where (and when) democracy is exercised in the form of elections is utterly dismal. It follows that anyone like Abou El Fadl who is searching for a tolerant Islam, an Islam that is not the Islam of a small group of unrepresentative voices, has only to look to the deliverance of democracy to find it. To find it one must—even as one writes essays reorienting our reading of a book along historically contextual lines—write and work toward the *democratization* of the political and civil environment of the people who claim the book as their own. If there is a failing of Islamic societies much more centrally relevant to the theme of tolerance than some offending verses in the Qur'an, it is this sustained absence of democratic mobilization; and at least some of the responsibility for this failing lies with the historical and contemporary influence of Europe and the United States, first by their colonial and then by their corporate presence in these Muslim nations.

INTOLERABLE INJUSTICES

MASHHOOD RIZVI

Never in history has violence been initiated by the oppressed. How could they be the initiators, if they themselves are the result of violence? How could they be the sponsors of something whose objective inauguration called forth their existence as oppressed? There would be no oppressed had there been no prior situation of violence to establish their subjugation. Violence is initiated by those who oppress, who exploit, who fail to recognize others as persons—not by those who are oppressed, exploited and unrecognized.

—Paulo Freire, *Pedagogy of the Oppressed*, 1972

Khaled Abou El Fadl's essay is an informative and successful demonstration of the central place of tolerance in Islam. But for the purposes of understanding the events of September 11 and their historical basis, such an analysis is premature and largely unnecessary. Indeed, it diverts attention from the real issues.

The events of September 11 had little to do with Islam; Islam and Muslims, especially those residing in the West, are instead now primarily victims of those events, as they face the wrath of zero-tolerance legislation and "homeland security" sweeps. (It is ironic that we are trying to spark a discourse on the place of tolerance in Islam while living in an age of "zero tolerance.") But September 11 has warned us of the devastating consequences of prolonged oppression and subjugation, while reminding us of the power of the human instinct for liberation.

It comes as no surprise that "the terrorist attacks on New York City and the Pentagon have focused public attention on the state of Muslim theology." By focusing on Islam, Western media outlets have distracted attention from the real geopolitical struggle. The Western media have dismissed any linkage between the horrific legacies of U.S. foreign policy on millions of people across the planet and the recent attacks on America. Instead they have celebrated U.S. "leadership." Abou El Fadl may be right that "for most Americans, the utter indifference to the value of human life and the unmitigated hostility to the United States shown by some Muslims came as a great shock." But one might ask these Americans why they have never felt shocked by the bombing "at will" of numerous defenseless, impoverished, and weak civilian populations; or by the appalling conditions of poverty and hunger that are, in so many ways, a direct result of their country's corporatized "development" efforts and plundering; or by the political cost-benefit analysis that categorizes children's lives in Iraq, Palestine, and Afghanistan as "expendable."

The world's most pressing problems do not result from either excessive or insufficient Islamic tolerance; nor are they a result of the caricatured portrait of Islam in the West and beyond—a portrait that has certainly tended to characterize Islam and all its followers as ignorant, brutal, confused, fundamentalist, and most recently "terrorists." Instead, and ultimately, the problem is the perpetuation of international systems of oppression and injustice.

According to the OED, oppression is "a prolonged harsh or cruel treatment or control." This phrase precisely describes the sustained misery experienced by vast numbers of us in the so-called Third World since the end of World War II. The gulf between rich and poor, unparalleled in world history, is no longer driven by purely economic interests. Instead it seems to be more a question of power: power to control and suppress, power to annihilate challenging ideas and provocative perspectives, especially those that might expose the grave injustices that shape our world. We are witnessing an age of monumental repression in which institutions of mass media and education play a strategic role in marginalizing opposition and manufacturing the consent necessary to sustain global political domination and economic pillage. The grim result is that most people in the world are now powerless to control their own affairs and unable to function as independent human beings.

Yet critical analysis of the current context must be accompanied by faith and hope for change. History is replete with examples of resistance and the reclamation of human dignity in the face of subjugation, from resistance to slavery, to the first battles against colonial invasion, to contemporary critiques of the instruments of indoctrination. In our time, a number of thinkers, leaders, and activists—Iqbal, Tagore, Shariati, Freire, Chomsky, and Said—represent the morality of the human spirit and its instinct for freedom. History teaches us that individual and collective consciousness form the core of optimism and fuel the struggle to challenge the forces of legitimized evil. As Iqbal puts it, "consciousness is the towering testament to the nobility of being human, which leads to an existence of disdain for materialism and to a genuine concern for others."

As an expression of that consciousness, Islam does not entail tolerance in shape of utter submission to callous acts of oppression and injustice. If the new push for tolerance in Islam means acceptance of oppression, then the most significant pillar of Islam—justice—will have to be set aside. The Qur'an states categorically that oppression is worse than slaughter: "fight them on until there is no more tumult or oppression and there prevails justice and faith in Allah but if they seize let there be no hostility except to those who practice oppression." I am not offering a religious justification for violent resistance. Those of us in the "developing" world are faced with daily horrors that should never be tolerated, with or without religious justification. Religious values and beliefs are certainly of use in helping oppressed peoples to separate the root problems from their symptoms. But at the end of the day, what one can and cannot tolerate is different for each of us.

The struggle between justice and tyranny cannot and should not be reduced to rich vs. poor, white vs. black or, for that matter, Islam vs. the West. Such dichotomies stand in the way of serious discussion, and distract us from the specific cultural and economic mechanisms that subjugate and bewilder our moral instincts. Controversies such as "tolerance in Islam" obscure the challenge that is revealed in the simple, yet profound moral capacities of human beings in the East and the West, and in their faiths: the vision of a just world.

STRUGGLE IN ISLAM

JOHN L. ESPOSITO

In the aftermath of September 11, Americans have had to face some hard questions: about global terrorism, the Muslim world, and our own country. "Is Islam more militant than other religions?" "Does the Qur'an condone violence and terrorism directed against nonbelievers?" "Is there a clash of civilizations between the West and the Muslim World?"

Khaled Abou El Fadl's brilliantly incisive article raises and addresses many of these fundamental issues. He describes with particular force a religious struggle for the soul of Islam between "puritanism" and modern Islam. The political side of this struggle is that a minority of extremists, who are dangerous and fanatical and thus predominate in media coverage, struggle against a majority that is often divided along a spectrum ranging from conservative to reformist. The situation is complicated by the nature of many Muslim governments—the Islamic authoritarian regimes, which limit dissent and rely on their military and security forces to stay in power. Failed states—politically and economically—and repression make for an explosive combination.

Of course religious revival and associated political conflict are not confined to the Islamic world. In recent years we have witnessed a global religious resurgence encompassing all major world religions. Personal piety has often been accompanied by political action in Israel, India, Sri Lanka, America, and much of the Muslim world. The majority of Islamic movements ("Islamic fundamentalists") have operated within their societies. But a minority have turned to violence and terrorism to overthrow regimes and impose their vision of an Islamic state. Like all religious extremists, militant Muslims exploit religion through selective reading and interpretation of sacred texts, history, and doctrine. Osama bin Laden and al-Qaeda appeal to grievances that exist among many mainstream Arabs and Muslims, from foreign policy issues like Palestine, the American presence in the Gulf, and the Russian presence in Chechnya, to domestic complaints against repressive and corrupt governments and failed economies. However, they transform Islam's norms and values—about good governance, social justice, and the requirement to defend Islam when under siege—into a call to arms, in order to legitimate the use of violence, warfare, and terrorism. Their theology or ideology divides the world into mutually exclusive categories: the world of belief and that of unbelief, the land of Islam and that of warfare, the forces of good and the forces of evil. Those who are not with them, whether Muslim or non-Muslim, are the enemy; they are to be fought and destroyed in a war with no limits, no proportionality of goal or means.

The situation has been compounded by governments that

have created and support a compliant religious establishment. Some religious leaders are seen as "lackeys" of the government, while many other *ulama* or religious scholars are seen as possessing a worldview and skills that are medieval and out of touch with the realities of modern Muslim life. They contribute to a worldview that is anti-reformist at best or one that promotes a militant exclusivist Islam and vision of the world. The spread of Wahhabi or Salafi Islam is a reflection of this problem.

Abou El Fadl represents a visible critical mass of Muslim intellectuals, laity, and clergy (*ulama*), men and women from Egypt to Indonesia. They emphasize the importance of reading texts within the historical and social contexts in which they were written. Distinguishing between universal principles and laws and texts that address specific time-bound issues, they explore major issues of modern reform: democratization, civil society, pluralism and tolerance, the status of minorities and women. The dialectic of change in the struggle between Puritanism and modern Islamic reform can be clearly seen in the debates over *democracy* and *jihad.*

In current debate about political participation, *secularists* argue for the separation of religion and the state. *Rejectionists* (both moderate and militant Muslims) maintain that Islam's forms of governance do not conform to democracy. King Fahd of Saudi Arabia, a longtime ally of the West, says that "the democratic system prevalent in the world is not appropriate in this region. . . . The election system has no place in the Islamic creed, which calls for a government of advice and consultation and for the shepherd's openness to his flock, and holds the ruler fully responsible before his people."[1] Extremists agree, condemning any form of democracy as *haram*, forbidden, an idolatrous threat to God's rule (divine sovereignty). Their unholy wars to topple governments aim to impose an authoritarian "Islamic" rule. Conservatives often argue that popular sovereignty contradicts the sovereignty of God, with the result that the alternative has often been some form of monarchy.

In contrast to both secularists and rejectionists, Islamic *reformers* have suggested ways to reinterpret key traditional Islamic concepts and institutions—consultation (*shura*) of rulers with those ruled, consensus (*ijma*) of the community, reinterpretation (*ijtihad*), and the public welfare (*maslaha*). They operate within Islam, and aim to show how Islamic ideas can be interpreted to support forms of parliamentary governance, representative elections, and religious reform. Just as it was appropriate in the past for Muhammad's senior Companions to constitute a consultative assembly (*majlis al-shura*) and to select or elect his successor (*caliph*) through a process of consultation, Muslims should now, according to these reformers, reinterpret and extend this notion to the creation of modern forms of political participation, parliamentary government, and the direct or indirect election of heads of state. The essential point, often missing from popular discussion, is that the debate about the virtues of democracy is not simply a debate *between* Islam and Western liberalism, but a debate *within* Islam itself.

Jihad provides a major example of this struggle within Islam. In the late-twentieth and early twenty-first century the word *jihad* has gained remarkable currency, becoming more global in its usage. On the one hand, *jihad*'s primary religious and spiritual meanings, the "struggle" or effort to follow God's path, to lead a good life, became more widespread. On the other hand, in response to European colonialism, authoritarian regimes, and other contemporary conditions, *jihad* has been used by resistance, liberation, and terrorist movements alike to legitimate their causes and motivate their followers. The Afghan Mujahiddin, the Taliban, and the Northern Alliance have all waged *jihads* in Afghanistan against foreign powers and among themselves; Muslims in Kashmir, Chechnya, Daghestan, the southern Philippines, Bosnia, and Kosovo have all fashioned their struggles as *jihads;* Hizbollah, HAMAS, and Islamic Jihad Palestine have characterized war with Israel as a *jihad;* the Armed Islamic Group has engaged in a *jihad* of terror against the Algerian government; and Osama bin Laden has waged a global *jihad* against Muslim governments and the West.

Today, the term *jihad* has become comprehensive; resistance/liberation struggles and militant campaigns, holy and unholy wars, are all declared to be *jihads. Jihad* is waged at home not only against unjust rulers in the Muslim world but also against a broad spectrum of civilians. *Jihad*'s scope abroad became chillingly clear in the 9/11 attacks, which targeted not only the American government but also innocent civilians.

Terrorists like bin Laden and others go beyond classical Islam's criteria for a just *jihad* and recognize no limits but their own, employing any weapons or means. They reject Islamic law's regulations regarding the goals and means of a valid *jihad*—that violence must be proportional and that only the necessary amount of force should be used to repel the enemy; that innocent civilians should not be targeted; and that *jihad* must be declared by the ruler or head of state. Today, individuals and groups, religious and lay, seize the right to declare and legitimate unholy wars in the name of Islam.

At the same time, Islamic scholars and religious leaders across the Muslim world—such as the Islamic Research Council at al-Azhar University, regarded by many as the highest moral authority in Islam—have made strong, authoritative declarations against bin Laden's initiatives: "Islam provides clear rules and ethical norms that forbid the killing of non-combatants, as well as women, children, and the elderly, and also forbids the pursuit of the enemy in defeat, the execution of those who surrender, the infliction of harm on prisoners of war, and the destruction of property that is not being used in the hostilities."[2]

As in the modern reform processes in Judaism and Christianity, questions of leadership and the authority of the past (tradition) are critical to both debates. Whose Islam? Who leads and decides? Is it rulers, the vast majority of whom are unelected kings, military, and former military? Or elected prime ministers and parliaments? Is it the *ulama* or clergy, who continue to see themselves as the primary interpreters of Islam, although many are ill-prepared to respond creatively to modern realities? Or is it modern, educated, Islamically oriented intellectuals like Abou El Fadl and others? Lacking an effective leadership, will other Osama bin Ladens fill the vacuum?

Moreover, there is the question: "What Islam?" Is Islamic reform simply a returning to the past and restoring past doctrines and laws, or is it a reformation or reformulation of basic Islamic ideas to meet the demands of modern life? Some call for an Islamic state based upon the re-implementation of classical formulations of Islamic laws. Others argue the need to reinterpret and reformulate law in light of the new realities of contemporary society.

As we pick up the pieces and move forward, Muslims face critical choices. If Western powers need to rethink and reassess their foreign policies and their support for authoritarian regimes, mainstream Muslims worldwide will need to address more aggressively the threat to Islam from religious extremists. The struggle for reform faces formidable obstacles: the conservatism of many (though not all) *ulama;* the traditional training of religious scholars and leaders; and the power of more puritanical, exclusivist Wahhabi or Salafi brands of Islam. To overcome these obstacles, this *jihad* for openness and renewal will need to move forward rapidly on religious, intellectual, spiritual, and moral fronts, and to embrace a wide-ranging process of reinterpretation (*ijtihad*) and reform.

PLURAL TRADITIONS

QAMAR-UL HUDA

The rising influence of extremists and literalists in world religions has been the center of fundamentalism studies for the past ten years, in large part due to the pioneering work gathered in Martin E. Marty and R. Scott Appleby's *The Fundamentalism Project*. Just as this collection reveals the social, political, economical, historical, and ideological roots of fundamentalism, Khaled Abou El Fadl's insightful essay explores the complexities of Islamic fundamentalism and its links with the history of puritanical Wahhabi and Salafi Islam. Just as *The Fundamentalist Project* helped to refine our understanding of "fundamentalism" despite some severe analytical weaknesses, Abou El Fadl offers an illuminating critique of the background assumptions behind Muslim extremist interpretations of the Qur'an, despite some weaknesses in his analytical frame.

Abou El Fadl accurately describes the ideological interconnections between contemporary Wahhabism, Jihad organizations, and Osama bin Laden's al-Qaeda group while exploring the struggle within the puritanical Islamic movement to assert the purest and most authentic form of Islam. This triangular relationship reveals an important dynamic among modern religious-political groups who aim to influence and reconstitute Muslim religious practices, politics, social customs, and identities; each player is involved with de-legitimizing the other purist as not strictly adhering to real Islam. Essentially, these groups are operating in a destructive cycle of hate, anger, power politics, and religious supremacy in order to establish a unique claim to be the true heirs of the authentic faith. They establish their authority principally by reading and interpreting with a narrow lens, by becoming expert in the rote recitation of Qur'anic verses, and by undermining tolerant Muslims and denouncing the faiths of non-Muslims.

Still, Abou El Fadl's discussion is based on a limited account of the historical realities of religious authority and scholarship. He correctly notes historical tensions between the state and religious scholars; however, his view is based on the traditional understanding of these tensions. Specifically, the standard view involves a vertical and a horizontal plane: the vertical plane is represented by the almighty state and its bureaucratic institutions, while the horizontal plane is represented by learned scholars of law, theology, philosophy, the sciences and others working under the state's patronage to ensure that law is enforced. Ordinary people, in turn, are connected to the Qur'an and directed to a better understanding of their religious law, customs, and histories by the generosity of state bureaucrats and scholars. In this standard model, we have an authority (the state), learned voices who represent the knowledge of the faith (scholars), and ordinary people, who are satisfied because they do not

need to think about religious issues because they are con-
sumed with daily secular matters.

Starting from these premises, Abou El Fadl draws the er-
roneous conclusion that "the state has co-opted the clergy,
and transformed them into its salaried employees. This
transformation has reduced the clergy's legitimacy, and produced a profound vacuum in religious authority. Hence,
there is a state of virtual anarchy in modern Islam: it is not
clear who speaks with authority on religious issues."

But the complexity and multiplicity of authorities in Islam is not a new phenomenon. To assert that religious authorities are now co-opted by the state is not to acknowledge
the intimate historical interplay between the two. From the
mid-eighth century onward, educational institutions and
the intellectual endeavor of Muslim scholars operated with
state patronage. But in addition to these trained scholars
(who were not "clergy" in any sense), there were a host of
learned spiritual teachers who were at times working in the
colleges (*madrasas*) or had established their own orders for
spiritual enlightenment, commonly referred to as Sufi orders. Since the tenth century, Sufis were scholars of law,
philosophy, theology, literature, medicine, mathematics,
and astronomy. Prominent Sufis like Abu Bakr al-Shibli (d.
946) and al-Qushayri (d.1074) were important scholars and
influential members in all of the major Sunni and Shi'a legal
schools (*madhabs*), and were major advisers to statesmen on
jurisprudence like Shaikh Abu Hafs 'Umar al-Suhrawardi
for the Abbassid caliph al-Nasir. It is widely known, too,

that Sufi scholars had developed their own ways of defining and transmitting spiritual knowledge and authority, and had simultaneously devised their own strategies for legitimization. Sufi scholars were not only accepted in mainstream Sunni Islam but were crucial in the intellectual growth and flourishing of Islamic scholarship. To not acknowledge these important voices of religious authority in the past and present is to ignore the traditional plurality of authorities in Islam, especially if these authorities do not situate themselves in the center of the state apparatus. The problem is not religious anarchy, as though an authoritative voice of Islam would be a good thing, but the lack of serious dialogue and consultation by Islamic states with a variety of Islamic authorities.

Finally, Abou El Fadl is misguided, I believe, in his consistent labeling of puritanical extremists' ideas as a "theology." Bin Laden's al-Qaeda and other Wahhabi Jihad groups are politically motivated reform movements with an injection of reductive religious slogans; they do not have theologies in the classical use of the word. In Islam, there is an illustrious tradition in the study of systematic theology (*kalam*) where faith is enriched by using the intellect and soul to better understand one's relationship with the divine, as in al-Kindi's (d. c.866) *Maq-lah fi'l 'Aql* ("On the Intellect"). From the earliest days of Islamic theology, *kalam* was intertwined with the rational philosophy and neo-Platonic ideas of the soul being derived from divine substance—for example, Abu Bakr al-Razi's (d. 925 or 935) *Sirah al-Falsafi-*

yah ("The Philosophical Way") and *al-Tibb al-Ruhani* ("The Spiritual Physician"). Even within this field of Islamic theology there was intense debate about whether rational philosophy is integral to *kalam* as with Andalusian Ibn Rushd (Averroes) and al-Ghazzali. If there was a point in history where rational theological ideas were first perceived harmful and irrelevant to Islamic jurisprudence it would not be with Muhammad ibn 'Abd al-Wahhab, as suggested by Abou El Fadl, but with Ibn Taymiyya and Ibn Hazm, who both rejected all forms of deduction, analogy, imitations (*taqlid*) in order to return to the ways of "the pious ancestors" (*al-salaf al-s-lih*). And this is why for many modern Wahhabi purists, Ibn Taymiyya is considered to be the father of their movement—although his thought has a far more complex view of metaphysics, Sufism and law than what contemporary Wahhabis would like us to believe. I think that Abou El Fadl gives them too much credit when he describes their way of defending divine law and their legally codified ethical values as a "theology"; it resembles a pseudo political-religious ideology more than a coherent religious doctrine.

A deeper understanding of Wahhabi purists and their splinter groups will enlighten us as to how they view the world and their place in it. What deserves more attention, however, is how tolerant Muslims around the globe will devise mechanisms to defend themselves from the extremist movements and to revitalize their own faith's traditions of cultivating openness, pluralism, and a compassionate heart and soul.

THE QUANDARY OF LEADERSHIP

R. SCOTT APPLEBY

In these anxious months following the atrocities of September 11, Muslims—indeed, all people of faith—are in desperate need of such courageous, erudite, humane, and serious scholars and public intellectuals as Khaled Abou El Fadl, a man who effortlessly inhabits both roles. His area of scholarly expertise—the history and contemporary interpretation and application of Islam's sacred sources—counts among the most pressing subjects of our time. Happily, God has given Abou El Fadl an intellect capable of mastering the complexities of Qur'anic and legal discourse, as well as the ability to convey to nonspecialists the substance of classical and modern jurisprudence, a topic most Westerners would otherwise find hopelessly esoteric.

Abou El Fadl goes directly to the heart of his topic—the place of tolerance in contemporary Islam—by identifying the structural problem underlying what we might call the narrowing of Islam, namely, a crisis of religious authority. Significantly, he describes "a major shift, unlike any [Islam] has experienced in the past." Strong and revealing words from an historian who recognizes the fact that "Islamic civilization has crumbled, and the traditional institutions that once sustained and propagated Islamic orthodoxy—and marginalized Islamic extremism—have been dismantled."

The comparative study of religious traditions demonstrates their fluidity over time, the inevitability of their adaptation to changing political and cultural circumstances, and the multiplicity of legitimate, if unreconciled, theological and religio-legal precedents that can become options for believers as they formulate responses to the challenges of the day. Islam, no less than Christianity, Judaism, Hinduism, or Buddhism, enjoys this "internal pluralism" of teachings, practices, and ethical responses. "Traditionally," as Abou El Fadl puts it, "Islamic epistemology tolerated and even celebrated divergent opinions and schools of thought."

By absorbing the once-independent religious scholars into the modern state system and thereby reducing them to a condition of dependence and timidity, Egypt, Saudi Arabia, and other putatively Muslim nations have created the conditions for the abandonment of the internal pluralism of Islam and the rise of the dramatic, violent, and vulgar contestation of the tradition by a technical class of engineers and their theologically third-rate clerical advisers. (Osama bin Laden is no shaykh, however often he refers to himself as such.) "Hence," Abou El Fadl rightly concludes, "there is a state of virtual anarchy in modern Islam: it is not clear who speaks with authority on religious issues."

In the essay under consideration, however, Abou El Fadl does not address the other side of the equation, namely, the impoverishment of the Islamic educational system and the growing religious illiteracy of the Muslim masses. By "religious illiteracy," I mean the lack of exposure to the great tradition of Islam—to the full range of authoritative responses, throughout the ages, to currently controverted questions such as the meaning of jihad, the proper conduct of a just war, the legitimate attitudes and behaviors toward non-Muslims, the appropriate means of redressing social and economic injustices, and so on. If reports are to be believed, young men studying in the madrasas are exposed only to the most militant and intolerant expressions of the tradition.

One must not indulge in sentimental and historically inaccurate nostalgia about past levels of religious literacy. Like the majority of lay Christians, the majority of lay Muslims were never fully fluent, to say the least, in the epistemological, legal, and theological discourses of their own religious tradition. Still, in our media-driven and state-dominated milieu, people take their cues, at an unprecedented rate, from "the other," rather than from their own sources of wisdom. The resulting vulgarization of Islam is extreme. Violence is mimetic and here the source of imitation is the brutal and bloody modern nation-state and/or the extremist guerrilla movements generated in symbiotic response to it. Christianity, Judaism, and Hinduism, no less than Islam, are held hostage in our times by "true believers," irony-stained "traditionalists" who have deeply inhaled the modern air of reaction, ideology, and mega-violence. They reach beyond the confines of the religious tradition in order to save it; in so doing, they weaken the tradition from within, making it all the more vulnerable to the forces of secularization.

In the case of Islam, the sorry educational and spiritual condition of the rank and file also reflects the displacement of independent jurists and competent religious scholars by do-it-yourself technocrats serving as self-appointed arbiters of the faith. For all contemporary faiths, the failures of religious formation and theological education have created a state of perplexity about modern religious leadership.

Traditional religious communities in the modern world require strong, independent, resolute leadership, capable of enabling the religious tradition to think and act on its own, apart from the corrupting influences of nationalist, irredentist, and other secular ideological currents. Christians, Jews, Muslims, Hindus, and Buddhists seek, and often clamor openly for, "authentic" religious leadership and self-evident authority. But authority has been hijacked by the purveyors of intolerance, hatred, and state-mimicking violence. Too many would-be followers do not seek nuanced and well-reasoned expositions of the religious law or binding precepts of the faith; instead they respond—from within a culture of retaliation and demonization of the enemy—to the fiery preacher, the ruffian who legitimates and channels their anger in "religious" terms.

Thus, Serbian Orthodox soldiers reportedly sang Christian hymns as they pillaged Bosnian towns and raped Muslim women. Extremist Jewish settlers invoke the Torah as they violate every sacred injunction against murder and hatred. Al-Qaeda terrorists, acting in the name of Islam, transgress prohibitions against the killing of innocents long established in Islamic law. The result is a tragic conflation of the law of the street with the law of the Gospel, the Torah, and the Qur'an.

My response, therefore, to Abou El Fadl's text on tolerance in Islam is fundamentally a response engaging Abou El Fadl himself—who he is, and what he has been willing to stand for in the open court of public opinion (at no small threat to his own well-being). The vital question facing Islam today is not "who ought to lead?" Now, as in every age, the answer to that question, for all religions, must be: The authoritative and authentic exemplars and masters of the religious tradition must lead—or, they must, at the least, exercise decisive influence over those who lead, teach, recruit, and shape ordinary believers. In other words, the pressing question for Islam today is a practical and political question: How can qualified jurists, religious scholars, and leading intellectuals like Abou El Fadl regain a place of authority over the masses within the house of Islam? How can they successfully contest the vulgar purveyors of a facile, expedient Islam that ultimately betrays the full wisdom of the tradition?

As outsiders to Islam, most Americans—Christian or otherwise—who have any depth of understanding of world affairs realize that a change in religious leadership, leading to a transformation of what Abou El Fadl calls "the more prevalent intellectual and theological currents in modern Islam," is absolutely necessary if the predicted "clash of civilizations" is to be avoided. While it turns on solving the institutional crisis affecting seminaries, religious colleges, and mosques, the battle over the soul of Islam, we recognize, is ultimately a spiritual contest. Aware that we cannot effectively intervene in this internal struggle, American Christians are watching anxiously as it unfolds.

The availability of multiple sanctioned paths to the one God, including a variety of interpretations of sacred writ, all seen within the range of orthodoxy, demonstrates that a religious tradition is using its collective mind—and heart—as God intended. Muslims and Catholics alike confess God to be the One beyond all comprehension, the One who encompasses, blesses, and transcends all our honest strivings toward God, and the One who nonetheless commands our obedience and continual striving. If this is so, then we must celebrate internal pluralism—regulated and bounded by the deliberations and witness of faithful jurists, theologians, mystics, prophets, gurus, and saints—as God's great gift to the believers.

May religious leaders who embrace the authority and possibilities of this gift multiply and prosper within all the great religious traditions.

3

REPLY

KHALED ABOU EL FADL

I begin my response to this remarkable collection of essays by recounting a rather unremarkable recent event. A few weeks ago, after once again enduring extra security screens, suspicious gazes, and anxiety about becoming the unwitting victim of a terrorist attack, I flew from Los Angeles to New York City, where I had been invited to deliver a lecture on the subject of tolerance in Islam. I used the opportunity to advocate what I called the "imperative of a collective enterprise of goodness." At the conclusion of the lecture, an older woman, who described herself as a New Yorker, stood up to speak; after a long diatribe, her question to me was: "After 9/11 and all that happened, as a Jew and a supporter of Israel, I have become scared of people who look like you—in truth, I am scared of you. So what can you say to make people like me feel safer?"

Although the woman's comment and question were certainly offensive, the incident is rather unremarkable because such occurrences are so common. All too often, Muslims living in the West experience the same level of ingrained hate, distrust, and racism. I, of course, refused to bear collective responsibility for the actions of a criminal few who happen to be Arab or Muslim. I felt I owed the woman no assurances—it was not my duty to alleviate her fears any more than it is the duty of any human being to console the anxieties of racists. Even more, what I could not explain, and what I suspect this woman could not understand, is that as a Muslim and an Arab I feared her.

I feared this woman not because I thought that she might incite violence against me personally. Rather, I feared her because she was unwittingly perpetuating a dynamic in which Muslims have been locked for the last couple of centuries. In demeanor and expression, she exemplified the stance that has doomed Muslims to ages of despair, distrust, degradation, and extremism: Western hostility, suspicion, and dismissiveness, which is reciprocated by Muslims in all the wrong ways. I had bared my heart in a lecture that treated the Islamic legal tradition with utter seriousness and indulged in wakeful humanistic dreams about a better future for all. Her response was pragmatic and functional: about who gets to feel safe in this world and how. In her worldview, when it comes to Muslims, none of the nuances mattered; she did not bother with the details. Instead, she focused on the bottom line of the functionality of Muslims—their utility or disutility—are Muslims dangerous or not?

Since the age of colonialism, this deprecating way of looking at Muslims has produced two main reactions, the first apologetic and the second defiant. Either Muslims have tried to prove their utility to the doubting other, or they responded by embracing the appearance of disutility. In other words, they either tried to ingratiate themselves to people like this woman, by assuring them that Muslims are harmless, or they have defiantly positioned themselves as the embodiment of this woman's worst nightmare. In either case, the intellectual history of Muslims in the post-colonial age has remained emotionally reactive with very little integrity or autonomy. Muslim thinking has remained either pro-West or anti-West instead of focusing on a far more important question: Is Muslim thinking in the modern world pro-human or anti-human—are the doctrinal assertions of modern Islam humane or inhumane?

WHAT ISLAM?

John Esposito aptly raises the most fundamental question confronting Muslims today: What Islam? Which of the many manifestations of Islam throughout history is to shape the moral import and meaning of this grand religious tradition? What will Muslims do with their past? How will they bring it to bear upon the present? How will Muslims relate to "the other"? This process of self-definition is complicated by both internal and external factors that contribute to the dearth of autonomy in the Muslim world. Internally, nearly all Muslim countries are governed by authoritarian regimes that stultify serious possibilities for free, vigorous discourse. Externally, Muslims are among the most powerless, dominated, and abused people in the world. This makes the question of tolerance particularly troublesome.

After all, isn't the real question whether non-Muslims are willing to tolerate Muslims, instead of the other way around? As Mashhood Rizvi and Abid Ullah Jan intimate, when it comes to Muslims, doesn't any discussion of tolerance translate into an acceptance of non-Muslim oppression and hegemony?

I think that Rizvi has a point and if one overlooks Jan's ad hominem attacks, he has a point as well. But, as noted above, the issue is not simply whether Muslims are able to resist foreign oppression. The point is the moral integrity of the Islamic tradition itself. My outrage about the terrorism of September 11 is not so much about supporting or protecting non-Muslims as such, as it is about defending the moral status and structure of the Islamic message. Islam is not, as Jan seems to treat it, simply a national or social identity; it is a monotheistic world religion. The Islamic religion expresses a universal message that speaks to humanity, but it must also construct a way of engaging humanity in a moral conversation and in a collective enterprise of moral goodness. However, what Amina Wadud appropriately describes as "extremist interpretive modalities" thoroughly frustrate the universalistic and humanistic message of Islam. When the average person in the world today associates the very word "Islam" with images of harshness, suffering, oppression, and violence, Islam becomes an idiosyncrasy—a moral and social oddity that is incapable of finding common ground with the rest of human society. As such, the real danger is that extremist interpretive modalities transform Islam into the outcast or the "other" that perhaps may be explained or interpreted, but not seriously engaged as a religious and moral outlook. In fact, I share Milton Viorst's concern that Muslims may become a "global underclass" living in a "social backwater." As Scott Appleby perceptively notes, the extremists of Islam are contributing to the vulgarization of the religion in such a way that its richness and humanism are becoming a distant memory. But as the case of the oil-rich Gulf states demonstrates, the threat is not simply economic. Extremist modalities of thinking are threatening to make the Islamic tradition a global intellectual delinquent.

I agree with Amina Wadud that extremists are as destructive within Muslim societies as they are in the non-Muslim world. For instance, the trauma that extremists inflict upon the women who make up half of the Islamic population is unconscionable. Extremism defines Islam in ways that make it thoroughly ugly in the eyes of anyone with a reasonable level of moral probity. Jan's response, for example, shows a striking lack of concern for the suffering inflicted on Muslims by these extremists. Jan and his cohort seem uninterested in the oppression of Muslim women or in the abysmal human rights record of such groups as the Taliban, as if it is acceptable that these so-called defenders of Islam victimize and degrade Muslims in pursuit of their goals. One wonders, in just what way, as Jan claims, do the likes of the Taliban and bin Laden exhibit "principled resistance" as they "stand up for justice even against their own self-interests"? Such claims can be sustained only if one completely ignores the Taliban's methodical brutalization of women, intellectuals, Shi'ites, and non-Pashtun tribal members, and the many innocent Muslims and non-Muslims who have been murdered by bin Laden in his glorious campaign of terror for justice.

But what of the fact that many Jewish and Hindu extremists brutalize and murder Muslims? Why should we speak of tolerance in Islam when the governments of the United States, Israel, India, Russia, and others consistently oppress and destroy Muslim communities while the world looks on? My response would be nearly identical to what I tell fellow Americans about responding to the terrorist acts of September 11. Terrorism aims to undermine the moral fiber of its victims. If Americans allow the attacks of September to alienate them from their moral values and from the civil liberties won in countless battles over two hundred years, then the terrorists have won. Similarly, if the Muslim response to the state terror inflicted upon them by Israel and other countries is to become alienated from their religious morality, then Muslims have lost something that is far more important than the political struggle—they have lost their moral grounding. As noted above, the ultimate issue for Muslims ought to be the moral integrity of the Islamic tradition. In my view, if the cost of any political or territorial victory is the loss of the Muslim ethical identity then the price is too high. This is not a call for political or even military pacifism.

This is simply an affirmation of the Qur'anic command to Muslims not to let the enmity or injustice of others become an excuse for the commission of further injustice.[1]

POLITICS AND INTERPRETATION

It should come as no surprise that those who, in the name of defending Islam, give primacy to political interests are also those most responsible for wreaking havoc with the Islamic tradition. Jan resents the fact that I speak about tolerance in Islam in the wake of September 11 and accuses me of opportunism and support for Islam-bashing. But tolerance is not a value invented by liberal Muslims in order to appease the West. Tolerance, known in Arabic as *tasamuh*, is a well-established Islamic value that has been debated at length for over a thousand years. Indeed, a whole category of Qur'anic verses pertaining to tolerance—known as *ayat al tasamuh*—ignited one of the richest debates in human history regarding the moral value of tolerance.[2] Interestingly, in the 1960s, the well-known Muslim jurist Muhammad al-Ghazali wrote an influential book on the tradition of tolerance in Islam.[3] If we follow Jan's logic, al-Ghazali, as well as any modern Muslim scholar who rekindles the norm of tolerance in Islam, was simply being an opportunist and trying to please the West.

But Jan does not merely aim to discredit individuals; he aims at nothing short of an abrogation of Qur'anic moral prescriptions themselves. Jan claims that the Qur'anic verse

5:69 was abrogated by verse 3:85, thus intimating that the tolerance displayed in the former verse was rendered null and void by the latter. Although this point might seem overly technical and even pedantic to non-Muslims, it raises a very important set of issues. According to the doctrine of abrogation, some rulings or determinations set out in the Qur'an can be annulled by subsequent Qur'anic rulings. The doctrine of abrogation thus expresses the idea of an incremental evolution of Qur'anic and Prophetic laws. However, the conditions, theory, and even possibility of abrogation of Qur'anic rulings were hotly debated topics in Islamic history.[4] Many jurists, most notably from the rationalist school, rejected the idea that the text of the Qur'an could contain verses whose meaning or import has been rendered null and void. Those jurists considered the doctrine of abrogation to be demeaning to the divine text because, in effect, it meant that parts of the Qur'an have been superseded, and therefore, are no longer of any use or relevance. Simply put, the doctrine of abrogation cannot simply be taken at face value.

Moreover, even the jurists who, in principle, accepted the doctrine of abrogation still disagreed about whether verse 5:69, in particular, was abrogated.[5] The issue, however, was much broader than verse 5:69. The real issue was the large number of Qur'anic verses that advocated tolerance and peaceful resolutions to conflict. For example, the message conveyed by 5:69 is reproduced verbatim in 2:62 and repeated in substance in several other verses.[6] It is unfortunate, in my view, that some classical jurists were willing to declare all Qur'anic verses that advocated tolerance, peace, or forgiveness to be abrogated by verses that prompted Muslims to fight the unbelievers. These jurists assumed a largely opportunistic logic in the construction of the Qur'an. Advocacy of tolerance and peace, according to these jurists, reflected the weakness of Muslims in the earliest phases of Islam. After Muslims became strong, tolerance or peaceful co-existence were no longer needed. This position verged on the absurd when some jurists declared that a single Qur'anic verse, which advocated fighting the unbelievers, abrogated 124 verses which called for tolerance and peace. Despite its influence on the modern puritans of Islam, this view met with disfavor among most classical jurists, who rejected its opportunistic logic and did not declare 5:69, or any similar verse, to be abrogated.[7]

The point here is not merely to salvage a particular verse of the Qur'an, although that is always a worthy cause, but to demonstrate the callous disregard with which many so-called defenders of Islam treat their tradition. Jan's essay conveys none of the Islamic tradition's nuance or complexity. From this perspective, Islam is devoid of any moral imperative other than a politically functional one. Instead of being critically and creatively engaged, the tradition becomes nothing more than a rubber stamp for whatever contemporary Muslims deem to be politically expedient.

Such political myopia is particularly apparent when it comes to questions of war and justice. While the Qur'an talks about *jihad* (struggling or striving in the way of God) as an inherently moral or good act, the Qur'an does not deal with *qital* (fighting or waging war) in the same way. It should be noted that in the Qur'an, every single reference to *qital* (fighting in a war) is qualified by some moral condition of restraint. Such moral restraint is often expressed in the form of a command to Muslims not to transgress and not to insist on using violence if there are credible avenues for achieving peace.[8]

Importantly, the Qur'an explicitly commands Muslims to fight only those who fight Muslims and to repel the injustice of others, but not to commit injustice themselves.[9] Classical Muslim jurists asserted that regardless of the justice of their cause, it would be considered an act of transgression for Muslims to attack or target noncombatants including children, women, seniors, or pacifists.[10] In addition, the classical jurists declared guerillas who attacked and terrorized civilians to be corrupters on the earth and criminals. They labeled such criminals as *muharibs,* which in this context meant criminals guilty of especially heinous crimes.[11] Contemporary dogmatists tend to ignore completely this aspect of the Islamic legal tradition. One notices that such dogmatists consistently seem to evaluate terrorism through the prism of international politics and nationalist aspirations, and *not* through the prism of Islamic moral thought. From the dogmatic perspective, injustices and immoralities committed by the likes of the Taliban or bin Laden are not seen as fundamental violations against Islam's moral tradition and are not treated seriously. Rather, such violations are treated as inconsequential in light of the struggle for higher political goals.

The Importance of Religious Morality

As this discussion demonstrates, the dilemmas of modern Muslim intellectuals are manifold. We must figure out how to deal with our own heritage, as well as with doubts about our own legitimacy and effectiveness. Stanley Kurtz, for example, somberly claims that the problem is that people like myself are not persuasive to Muslims in the Middle East. Our moral paradigms and interpretations only appeal to Muslims living in the liberal and secular West. In addition, both Tariq Ali and Kurtz, while suggesting that our efforts are laudable, assert that Muslim fundamentalism can be explained by material, sociopolitical conditions, and not by ideology. Ali seems to doubt the role of religion itself, presenting it as a reactionary element that primarily contributes to fanaticism and violence. In fact, Ali closes his essay with the startling claim that theology is useless.

In many ways, my exchange with Jan might be seen to confirm the suspicions of both Kurtz and Ali. It seems that Jan and I are firmly situated in our very different sociopolitical contexts, and that a considerable number of Muslims, living in underdeveloped and despotic states, are bent on defending reactionary and fanatic movements such as the Taliban.

This is not the place to challenge materialist interpretations of history or the notion that religious theologies always contribute to fanaticism and violence. I will only note that human beings seem capable of the most ugly fanaticism and violence without the contributions of religion. The ideologies and practices of nationalism, colonialism, communism, fascism, and corporatism contributed to destruction of life at least as much as religion ever has. In addition, I believe that Muslims such as the Taliban, who carry the banner of Islamic authenticity and legitimacy, are far more anti-Western than they are pro-Islamic. In many ways, they are not the outgrowth of a religious process, as much as a reaction to external secular forces, such as colonialism or corporate capitalism. One reason for engaging in theological thinking is to deny such groups their Islamic banner and to challenge their claim to authenticity.

But while I do not believe that theology is useless, I do think that it must be engaged in light of moral humanistic commitments. I would contend that these commitments are crucial to establishing any possibility of a good life. As a believer, my own humanistic moral vision does not and cannot exclude God as an active and real participant in the affairs of being. As a believer, I would go further and assert that a just and good life is not possible without acknowledging the company and participation of God. Millions of human beings, justifiably in my opinion, acknowledge God as part of their moral and material universe. This is why theology matters. If theology does not matter, then they do not matter, and, ultimately, I do not matter either. It would seem to me to be both unwise and immoral to imply that the perspectives of people whose theology is inseparable from their very existence simply do not matter. Furthermore, I do think that for both practical and principled reasons there is no alternative to engaging theology and working to change people's minds. Whether, as Kurtz seems to believe, socioeconomic conditions will inevitably prevent the spread of certain humanistic ideas, only time can tell. But for a believer there is simply no alternative but to try and then try again.

Interpreting the Islamic Tradition

Some of the challenges raised by the respondents in this book relate not so much to the plausibility of my objectives, but to my method of dealing with the Islamic tradition. First, I must note my agreement with Amina Wadud's insight that the text, especially that of the Qur'an, can enrich the reader far more than the reader can enrich the text. In many ways, the final line of defense against extremism is the text of the Qur'an itself. However, as Sohail Hashmi appropriately points out, interpretive communities do form around texts and at times they may hold the moral insights of the text hostage. Interpretive communities can stultify and imprison the text in an extremist paradigm that becomes very difficult to disentangle or dismantle and as a result makes it very difficult to restore the text's integrity. Regardless of what sociopolitical conditions contributed to the emergence of the contemporary puritans of Islam, the fear is that they will come to impose exactly such an extremist paradigm upon the whole of the Islamic tradition.

However, to the extent that Hashmi suggests that the juristic interpretive communities of the past were necessarily conservative, intolerant, or extremist, I disagree with him. Furthermore, I disagree with the attempt to locate the creative momentum of Islam largely in the Mu'azilite or Sufi traditions, as Milton Viorst and Qamar-ul Huda seem to do. It is an unjustifiable simplification to claim that Islamic intellectual development stalled in the tenth century, or that Muslim jurists were co-opted by the state and neutralized for most of Islamic history. While I agree with Huda that inadequate attention has been afforded to the contributions of the Sufi tradition, I dispute the claim that the intellectual endeavors of Muslim scholars were patronized by the state from the middle of the eighth century onward. I believe these conclusions reveal a level of dogmatic involvement with Islamic history and a serious misunderstanding of the dynamic and often dialectical development of Islamic juristic discourse until the sixteenth century at least.

Nevertheless, whatever the exact relationship between the juristic class and the state, the important point for today's Muslims is the nature of the scholastic heritage primarily found in the musty books of tradition. On this, I can confidently report that the one truly remarkable thing about classical Islamic scholarship is that, for its age and time, it was dynamic, diverse, complex, and constantly evolving well beyond the tenth century. In fact, for every dogmatic and intolerant voice found in the classical tradition, one can locate contemporaneous voices that challenged and refuted it. The reality is that when compared to the puritans of modern Islam, classical Muslim scholars look like raving liberals. In contemporary Islam, the problem is not the text but the reader. In most cases, the Islamic heritage is lost between analytically competent readers who are woefully incapable of penetrating the classical texts and readers who can decipher the classical texts, but who live in a time warp and are largely oblivious to the hermeneutic and analytic strategies of modern scholars. Put simply, the first group is equipped to handle modernity, but not the classical tradition, while the second group is in precisely the opposite position. This dilemma ought to be recognized as the real tragedy of modern Islamic scholarship.

To be sure, Hashmi and Akeel Bilgrami make a very important contribution in their refusal to sanctify and rarify the past. I think that as Muslim intellectuals, we must accept that the morality of the Qur'an exceeded the morality of its interpreters. In many respects, the Qur'anic text set moral trajectories that could not be adequately realized or even understood by the interpretive communities of the past. At times, the interpreters of the tradition completely missed the moral point of the Qur'anic message and generated determinations that locked the Qur'an into a shortsighted and inadequate sphere of meaning. But I think Wadud also makes a significant point here. As Muslims, we adhere to the religious conviction that the morality of the Qur'an will always exceed the morality of its interpreters. In other words, I do not believe that human beings can claim to have understood the message of the Qur'an perfectly and completely. Falling short of the Qur'an's moral message is inevitable, but it is also an impetus to engage in a never-ending dynamic of moral exploration and interpretation. As far as the interpretations of the past are concerned, the challenge confronting Muslim intellectuals is how to critically engage the interpretive traditions of the past without falling into the intellectually arrogant and historically myopic view that anything produced in modernity is necessarily morally superior to anything produced in the past. In addition, part of the difficulty is to articulate coherent and systematic moral theories that can help us both sift through the sands of past interpretation and to develop new interpretations of the text.

I do not support Bilgrami's conclusion that the solution is simply democratic politics. Politically, I tend to believe in constitutionalism, in limited government, and in individual and collective rights held against the state and others. But I am also suspicious of majoritarian systems of government and would suggest that much of the political rhetoric in democracies is vacuous at best. It's far from obvious that such a politics is adequate to resolve the crisis of religious authority that Islam faces. I do consider this an issue worthy of serious discussion, but it must be deferred to another context simply because of its enormity.

I do think it is very important, however, to comment briefly on another enormous issue that Bilgrami raises: the relationship in Islam between the Meccan and Medinian historical episodes. Jan makes the largely vacuous claim that the Prophet was sent to establish an Islamic government. For Jan, the culmination of the Prophet's message was the Medina period, when he established a city-state governed by *shari'a* law. Everything that happened in Mecca was simply prelude and thus Jan is able to dogmatically proclaim the historical experience and even the Qur'anic verses of the Meccan period to have been abrogated. Bilgrami, meanwhile, takes the exact opposite view; for him, it is the Meccan period that really embodied the Islamic message. Thus the Medinian period was far more about the exigencies of historical circumstance and institutional survival than about the revelation of Islamic normative principles. While I think Jan's position is largely anachronistic and disturbingly reductionist, I worry that Bilgrami's approach is theologically unjustifiable and that it ultimately discards too much of the Islamic experience.

First, it is important to note that contrary to what Bilgrami and others (such as Abdullahi An-Naim and many Western scholars) seem to think, it is not possible to clearly differentiate between the Qur'anic verses revealed in Mecca and those revealed in Medina. What was revealed when and why was as vigorously debated by the classical jurists as many subsequent incidents in Islamic history.

Second, much of what we suspect to have been revealed

or experienced in Medina contains moral principles that are at the very core of the Islamic approach to justice. In addition, the Medina period embodies many demonstrative examples of the actual application of the moral principles set out in the Mecca period.

Third, and most important, the bifurcation of the Mecca and Medina periods seems to obscure the most important point. The relevant issue is not what was revealed when and where, but what the primary principles of Islamic justice are and what principles are derivative or secondary. The important issue is to determine what might be called the hierarchy of Islamic values, and to ensure that a derivative or secondary value does not end up abrogating or voiding a primary value. For example, an Islamic government is not an end in itself. It is simply a means to the ultimate end: justice. Therefore, the issue ought to be how does one establish justice, not how to establish an Islamic government, regardless of its ability to support justice. This is what the classical jurists called an inquiry into *awlawiyyat al-Islam* (the priorities of Islam), and, unfortunately, it is another largely forgotten part of the Islamic intellectual heritage.

A MORAL TRUST

I am extremely grateful to the participants in this discussion. Bloodshed and suffering often acts as the impetus for human beings to start talking with one another, although ideally it should not be so. I wrote the opening essay on tolerance in Islam out of my deep concern for the Islamic tradition and my unwavering conviction that I belong to a great moral humanistic tradition. My purpose, as an Arab Muslim, was not to investigate the traditions of the non-Muslim West or to seek comfort in escapist platitudes of victimization or the destructiveness of angry self-pity. As a Muslim intellectual, I have no moral choice but to confront the following question: Do the bin Ladens of the Muslim world actually find justification for the ugliness that they perpetuate in any interpretive tradition in Islam? Does this level of intolerance and criminality find support, regardless of how flimsy or absurd, in some of the traditional interpretations? I think that, unfortunately, the answer must be yes—it would be dishonest to say otherwise. But fortunately, Muslims have the power to deconstruct and reject those interpretations.

God relegated to Muslims a moral trust. At no point in history can Muslims ignore their unending obligations to appropriately discharge this moral trust. The basic and invariable point is that Muslims—and non-Muslims—must understand that it is in the power and is in fact the duty of Muslims of every generation to answer the question: What Islam? The response must not be left in the hands of the bin Ladens of the world.

NOTES

KHALED ABOU EL FADL / *The Place of Tolerance in Islam*

1. Muhammad Amin Ibn 'Abidin, *Hashiyat Radd al-Muhtar* (Cairo: Mustafa al-Babi 1966), 6:413; Ahmad al-Sawi, *Hashiyat al-Sawi 'ala Tafsir al-Jalalayn* (Beirut: Dar Ihya al-Turath al-Arabi, n.d.), 3:307–308. See also Ahmad Dallal, "The Origins and Objectives of Islamic Revivalist Thought, 1750–1850," *Journal of the American Oriental Society* 113/3 (1993), who demonstrates that Wahhabism in the nineteenth century was considered a fringe fanatic group.

2. Qur'an 5:51.
3. Qur'an 3:85.
4. Qur'an 8:39.
5. Qur'an 9:29.
6. Qur'an 4:135.
7. Qur'an 49:13.
8. Qur'an 11:118–9.
9. Qur'an 5:49.
10. Qur'an 5:69; 2:62.
11. Qur'an 2:256; 10:99; 18:29.
12. Qur'an 2:190; 5:2.
13. Qur'an 2:194.
14. Qur'an 60:9.
15. Qur'an 8:61.
16. Qur'an 4:90. Also 4:94.

17. Abu Zakariyya al-Nawawi, *Rawdat al-Talibin*, ed. Zuhayr al-Shawish, 3rd ed. (Beirut: al-Maktab al-Islami, 1991), 10:316–7.

Sohail H. Hashmi / *A Conservative Legacy*

1. Muhammad ibn Ahmad al-Qurtubi, *al-Jami' li ahkam al-Qur'an,* vol. 2 (Cairo: Dar al-Katib al-'Arabi, 1967), 299; translated by Mahmoud Ayoub, *The Qur'an and Its Interpreters,* vol. 1 (Albany: State University of New York Press, 1984), 265.

2. Jane Dammen McAuliffe, *Qur'anic Christians: An Analysis of Classical and Modern Exegesis* (Cambridge: Cambridge University Press, 1991), 111.

3. Isma'il ibn 'Umar ibn Kathir, *Tafsir al-Qur'an al-'azim,* vol. 2 (Beirut: Dar al-Andalus, 1966), 589; Cf. Muhammad ibn Jarir al-Tabari, *Jami' al-bayan 'an tawil ay al-Qur'an,* vol. 3 (Damascus: Dar al-Qalam, 1997), 248.

Abid Ullah Jan / *The Limits of Tolerance*

1. Ibn 'Abbas, *Tafsir At-Tabari,* vol. 1, 323.

2. Qur'an 4:170.

3. Qur'an, 4:150–1. Also see Ay'at, 3:31–2, 4:69, 47:33, 24:52, 5:104, 7:157–8, 33:40, 61:6, and so forth.

John L. Esposito / *Struggle in Islam*

1. *Mideast Mirror,* 30 March 1992, 12.

2. *Al-Hayat,* 5 November 2001.

Khaled Abou El Fadl / *Reply*

1. Qur'an 5:8.

2. For examples of such verses, see 2:109; 5:13; 15:85; 24:22; 43:89; 64:14.

3. Muhammad al-Ghazali, *al-Ta'assub wa al-Tasamuh bayn al-Masihiyya wa al-Islam* [*Intolerance and Tolerance in Christianity and Islam*] (Cairo: Matba'at Hassan, n.d.).

4. For example, the medieval jurist al-Nahhas claimed that eighteen Qur'anic verses were abrogated; Makki claimed about thirty verses; Ibn al-Jawzi claimed nineteen verses.

5. Fakhr al-Din al-Razi, *al-Tafsir al-Kabir* (Beirut: Dar al-Kutub al-'Ilmiyya, 1990), 3:98 notes that it was not abrogated. Abu 'Abdullah al-Qurtubi, *al-Jami' li Ahkam al-Qur'an* (Cairo: Dar al-Ma'rifa, n.d.), 1:436, notes that there is disagreement on whether the verse was abrogated. Abu Muhammad Makki al-Qaysi, *al-Idah li-Nasikh al-Qur'an wa Mansukhuh* (Jedda: Dar al-Manarah, 1986), 123 asserts that most jurists agreed that this verse is not abrogated. Mustafa al-Maraghi, *Tafsir al-Maraghi* (Beirut: Dar al-Kutub al-'Ilmiyya, 1998), 1:116, argues that this verse means that non-Muslims who never had the opportunity to learn Islam in the correct way have an excuse before God and if they do good, they will be rewarded.

6. For example, 2:83; 2:256; 5:43, 47–8; 10:99; 11:118; 15:85; 18:29.

7. Abu Ja'far al-Nahhas, *al-Nasikh wa al-Mansukh* (Beirut: Mu'assasat al-Risalah, 1991), 1:338–9; Abu Ja'far al-Khazarji, *Nafasu al-Sabah* (Rabat, Morocco: Wizarat al-Awqaf, 1994), 1:196.

8. Qur'an 2:190–3, 208, 216, 246; 4:89–91, 191; 4:89–94; 8:39, 61; 9:36; 22:39; 33:25; 60:8–9.

9. Qur'an 5:2, 8; 2:191.

10. Fakhr al-Din al Razi, *al Tafsir al Kabir* (Beirut: Dar al-Kutub al-'Ilmiyya, 1990), 5:109 10; Abu Bakr al-Jassas, *Ahkam al-Qur'an* (Cairo: al-Awqaf al-Islamiyya, 1986), 1:256 7; Abu 'Abd Allah al-Qurtubi, al-*Jami' li-Ahkam al-Qur'an* (Cairo: Dar al-Kutub, 1954).

11. On this subject, see Khaled Abou El Fadl, *Rebellion and Violence in Islamic Law* (Cambridge: Cambridge University Press, 2001)

ABOUT THE CONTRIBUTORS

KHALED ABOU EL FADL is Omar and Azmeralda Alfi Distinguished Fellow in Islamic Law at UCLA and author of *Rebellion and Violence in Islamic Law*.

TARIQ ALI is author of *The Clash of Fundamentalisms: Crusades, Jihads and Modernity*. He is an editor at *New Left Review* and has written extensively on history and politics.

R. SCOTT APPLEBY is professor of history and director of the Institute for International Peace Studies at the University of Notre Dame. He is author of *The Ambivalence of the Sacred: Religion, Violence and Reconciliation*.

AKEEL BILGRAMI is Johnsonian Professor of Philosophy at Columbia University. His book *Politics and the Moral Psychology of Identity* will be published in 2003.

JOSHUA COHEN is Leon and Anne Goldberg Professor of the Humanities at MIT and editor in chief of *Boston Review*.

JOHN L. ESPOSITO is director of the Center for Muslim-Christian Understanding at Georgetown University, and author of *Unholy War: Terror in the Name of Islam*.

SOHAIL HASHMI is Alumnae Foundation Associate Professor of International Relations at Mount Holyoke College.

QAMAR-UL HUDA is professor of Islamic Studies and Comparative Theology at Boston College and author of *Striving for Divine Union: Spiritual Exercises for Suhrawardi Sufis*.

ABID ULLAH JAN is a political analyst and executive director of the Independent Centre for Strategic Studies (ICSS) in Peshawar, Pakistan.

STANLEY KURTZ is a research fellow at the Hoover Institution at Stanford University. He is a social anthropologist and has taught at Harvard University and the University of Chicago.

ABOUT THE CONTRIBUTORS

IAN LAGUE is a writer and editor living in San Francisco and former managing editor of *Boston Review*.

MASHOOD RIZVI is editor-in-chief of *EDucate! Educating for Social Change*, a quarterly magazine published by the Sindh Education Foundation, based in Karachi, Pakistan.

MILTON VIORST is the author of *In the Shadow of the Prophet: The Struggle for the Soul of Islam*.

AMINA WADUD is professor of Islamic studies at Virginia Commonwealth University and author of *Qur'an and Woman: Rereading the Sacred Text from a Woman's Perspective*.